Guide
to
Bicycle
Trails

ROBERT COLWELL'S

Guide to Bicycle Trails

Stackpole Books

GUIDE TO BICYCLE TRAILS

Copyright © 1974 by
Robert Colwell

Published by
STACKPOLE BOOKS
Cameron and Kelker Streets
Harrisburg, Pa. 17105

Printed in the U.S.A.

Library of Congress Cataloging in Publication Data

Colwell, Robert.
  Guide to bicycle trails.

  1. Cycling—United States. I. Title.
GV1045.C63   1974   796.6   74-4010
ISBN 0-8117-0768-7
ISBN 0-8117-2027-6 (pbk.)

CONTENTS

Seeing America on two wheels. Getting into the land.
Biking for health and recreation. 90 million Americans
are right! Young and old. Our changing roads: more
traffic on the interstate systems. Our secondary roads are
quieter. Bike routes: types and description. Bicycle touring
and its increasing popularity. Guided tours. Centennials.
Choosing a touring bike. Accessories. Getting you and your
bike to the start and back home. Safety on the road. The
need filled by this book. How trails were chosen. How
they were rated. How to use this book. Reference matter.
Organizations and their addresses. Books of interest. Publications with up-to-date information. Maps and guides.

VERMONT—small towns, well kept farms, scenic country-side and lightly traveled roads. TOUR 22 is a good view of pastoral Vermont. TOUR 23 is a tough loop through the mountains of southern Vermont.

Chapter 4   TRAILS MIDWEST   139

ILLINOIS—delta country touring in southern Illinois on TOUR 24.

INDIANA—TOUR 25 along the Ohio River to Madison is a pleasant outing.

MICHIGAN—in a vacation state like Michigan there are unlimited touring possibilities. TOUR 26 is a shoreline route along Lake Huron with a visit to Ft. Michilimackinac. TOUR 27 takes you along Lake Michigan and through charming towns like Leland and Northport.

OHIO—once away from urban centers bikers will find the Ohio countryside inviting. TOUR 28 is a hilltop route highlighted by a visit to restored Roscoe Village. TOUR 29 includes a section of the famous TOSRV outing. TOUR 30 is a difficult outing among the hills and forests of south-central Ohio.

WISCONSIN—dairy farms, orchards, rolling hills and breezy lakeshore country for bikers who like pastoral settings for their outings. TOUR 31 runs out onto the peninsula northeast of Green Bay. TOUR 32 includes hill biking and an excursion into Illinois where a visit to Galena is a must.

Chapter 5   TRAILS WEST   177

ARIZONA—spectacles like the Grand Canyon and a bloom-ing desert in spring are solid attractions for bikers in Arizona. TOUR 33 loops out of Flagstaff to Sunset Crater, the Wupatki Ruins and the Grand Canyon.

CALIFORNIA—just about any climate and terrain available here, and much of it year-round biking. TOUR 34 is the long run down the coast from San Francisco to Morro Bay. TOUR 35 rises into the Sequoia National Park amongst the giant trees. TOUR 36 includes mesa biking and a climb to scenic Lassen Peak. TOUR 37 runs through valleys of orchards and vineyards before touching the coast.

NEW MEXICO—tours here can include visits to Indian ruins, charming towns like Santa Fe and the rugged wilder-ness of the Sangre de Cristo Mountains. TOUR 38 loops into Colorado, where a stop in Durango might include a scenic railroad trip through the San Juan Mountains.

OREGON—the seashore, the Cascades and the rolling hills between. Camping facilities are about the best in the coun-try. TOUR 39 runs north on an easy route to Crater Lake;

then it gets tougher. TOUR 40 is a very scenic ride through northwestern Oregon with some time on the coast.

WASHINGTON—anywhere in this state is good summer biking. TOUR 41 includes a ride up and around Mt. Rainier. TOUR 42 is a loop around the Olympic Peninsula. TOUR 43 traces some of the Lewis and Clark route along the Columbia River to the coast.

WYOMING—mountain splendor, vast grazing lands and a mean elevation above 1 mile makes this an attractive biking state. TOUR 44 takes you through the Grand Teton and Yellowstone National Parks. TOUR 45 is an extension for the hardy bikers.

CITY—TRAIL INDEX
Finding Bicycle Trails Near a City

In selecting bicycle trails for this book, consideration was given to their proximity to urban areas. With each city in the following index are listed by tour number those bicycle trails within a 125-mile radius, or about 3 hour's driving time from a city. In some cases the radius has been stretched. This index includes over 140 cities, 102 of which have been selected from the 150 cities in America with populations over 100,000.

BEAUMONT, Texas—Tour 9
BEND, Oregon—Tours 39, 40
BERKELEY, California—Tours 34, 35, 37
BILLINGS, Montana—Tours 44, 45
BIRMINGHAM, Alabama—Tours 3, 5
BOSTON, Massachusetts—Tours 10, 12, 13, 14, 15, 18, 22, 23
BRIDGEPORT, Connecticut—Tours 12, 13, 14, 16, 8, 23
BUFFALO, New York—Tours 17, 20, 21
BUTTE, Montana—Tours 44, 45
CAMDEN, New Jersey—Tours 4, 16, 20
CANTON, Ohio—Tours 19, 21, 28, 29, 30
CEDAR RAPIDS, Iowa—Tour 32
CAMBRIDGE, Massachusetts—Tours 10, 12, 13, 14, 15, 18, 22, 23
CHARLESTON, West Virginia—Tours 19, 25, 28, 29, 30
CHARLOTTE, North Carolina—Tours 5, 6, 7
CHATTANOOGA, Tennessee—Tours 3, 5
CHICAGO, Illinois—Tours 31, 32
CINCINNATI, Ohio—Tours 25, 28, 29, 30
CLEVELAND, Ohio—Tours 19, 21, 28, 29, 30
COLUMBIA, South Carolina—Tours 3, 5
COLUMBUS, Georgia—Tours 3, 5
COLUMBUS, Ohio—Tours 25, 28, 29, 30
CONCORD, New Hampshire—Tours 10, 11, 12, 13, 14, 15, 18, 22, 23
DALLAS, Texas—Tour 9
DAYTON, Ohio—Tours 25, 28, 29, 30
DAYTONA BEACH, Florida—Tours 1, 2
DEARBORN, Michigan—Tours 26, 27, 28
DETROIT, Michigan—Tours 26, 27, 28
DUBUQUE, Iowa—Tours 31, 32
DURANGO, Colorado—Tour 38
ELIZABETH, New Jersey—Tours 4, 13, 16, 18, 20, 22
ELMIRA, New York—Tours 16, 17, 18, 20, 21
ERIE, Pennsylvania—Tours 17, 19, 20, 21, 28
EUGENE, Oregon—Tours 39, 40
EUREKA, California—Tours 36, 37
EVANSVILLE, Indiana—Tours 24, 25
FARMINGTON, New Mexico—Tour 38
FLAGSTAFF, Arizona—Tour 33
FLINT, Michigan—Tours 26, 27
FT. WAYNE, Indiana—Tours 25, 28, 29, 30
FREMONT, California—Tours 34, 35, 37
FRESNO, California—Tours. 34, 35
GLENS FALLS, New York—Tours 13, 14, 15, 16, 17, 18, 22, 23
GRAND RAPIDS, Michigan—Tours 26, 27
GRANTS PASS, Oregon—Tour 39

INTRODUCTION

THERE IS SOMETHING remarkable about bike tourers. This is especially so of those singular ones who take to the road alone or with a companion or two. To some extent they are testing their skills and resources much the same as do backpackers, wilderness canoeists and ski tourers; their involvement is as intimate and physical. And like canoeists and ski tourers they have learned to manage their mechanical assists. Combining a desire to get out and see the land with their need for mobility, their efforts lead them to wonderful and lasting experiences.

Fortunately our natures allow us to quickly forget the spills, the traffic, the rain, the heat, and the grueling struggle against headwinds. Rather we remember the giddy downhill runs, the wind tugging at our hats and shirts, the cool respite from a hot sun. We delight in savoring the summer smells of wildflowers, fresh cut hay, barnyards, and pines in shady forest routes. Our spirits are tuned to the music of insects' buzz and whine, of songbirds at roadside and distant, cawing crows. We find ourselves easily enthralled with the indescribable peace and contentment when, on a lonely road, we stop to gaze out across rolling hills or a quiet pond.

This book is written for those people who like touring to be an individual experience rather than a group outing. This book is also for those who have, in the past, enjoyed larger outings and now want to go it alone, biking different parts of our land over trails that are exciting and challenging.

CHAPTER 1

SEEING AMERICA
ON TWO WHEELS

SEEING AMERICA ON two wheels is becoming increasingly popular. Whether it is a short ride that reveals more of a neighborhood or town, or a long tour that follows country roads to scenic splendor, it is an excellent way to "get into" our land. Biking offers the mobility of the auto, yet with the sensible speeds needed to really see and enjoy the countryside. While it is not the same as hiking, in terms of visual involvement, neither is it as limiting in distance covered.

BIKING FOR HEALTH AND RECREATION

Like so many other outdoor activities biking is for those who like a non-competitive leisurely pastime. And it is enjoyed by a broad age spectrum that is more apparent here than in any other outdoor activity. Over 90 million Americans are on bicycles, youngsters and oldsters, and their numbers continue to increase. This is particularly true of adult bikers. For years parents have bought bikes for their kids only, but things have changed! Now we see adults carrying their own bikes along

Cascade peaks in Oregon.

with their childrens', headed out for a vacation or a weekend away from the city.

And adults have become bike commuters. It's been proven that in some cities a biker can beat the traffic problems. While it may take a rather fearless outlook, the exercise and fun are worth the effort and challenge. These same adult bikers are the main participants in a new and exciting part of bicycling: bike touring. Bikers in couples, small parties and large organized groups are seeing the land in a fashion seldom thought of a few years ago.

OUR CHANGING ROADS

This new interest in biking has paralleled the change in the use of our road system. The changes have been good for the biker in one sense. Even though the auto population increases, a lot of secondary roads see less of them now that traffic is being channeled into the interstate system and improved major highways. However, in and around urban areas the problem worsens.

Often it is a case of having to drive some distance to a jump-off point for biking—even an evening ride! Those bikers who live in quiet suburban areas will always enjoy casual outings, but most of those remain rather short routes. We must increasingly look to our secondary rural roads for our biking trails, long and short.

BIKE ROUTES

At present no criteria is universally used to describe bicycle routes. Many names have been used: bikeways, bike paths, bike routes, bike trails, bike lanes, etc. However, few people are aware of the difference in the meanings of these names. Perhaps the confusion stems from adopted ideas of their meaning, which vary, from biker to biker, club to club and so on. For some a bikeway is a very definite, restricted route for the biker or hiker only. For others it is simply a route through a town with signs showing the way. Below are a list of the names most often used and an explanation of what this writer has known them to mean.

Bikeway: designated route for bicycles (towpath, railbed or abandoned road) sometimes shared with hikers and horseback riders.

Bike Path: similar to the above, but on a smaller scale such as in a park.

Bike Route: most common designation; urban, suburban streets signed to direct.

Bike Lane: designated lane paralleling auto traffic, generally in urban areas where commuters have turned to bicycles.

Bike Trail: usually associated with long tours through the countryside, mostly over secondary roads.

BICYCLE TOURING

Bicycle touring is the heart of this book. Its popularity amongst the adult population and young people has increased phenomenally in the last few years. This interest is reflected in the booming sales of the vari-speed bikes, the most popular being the 10-speed bike that allows us to make short mileage of those long trips and easy hills out of some steep ones. With one of these bikes, touring can be very enjoyable.

Many bikers tour on their own or with friends. Others get their first taste of touring with one of the larger outings sponsored by bicycle clubs and organizations. These guided tours fall into two categories. The most familiar is the club outing, conducted by a leader and always over a route already scouted and biked at another time. It may be a short ride to a favorite historical site or point of interest in the area. More often they are just pleasant riding routes in a scenic setting. Many of these tours are annual events. Sag wagons often accompany these outings, bringing up the rear while carrying excess luggage, refreshments, and those few bikers who cannot keep the pace.

The bike tour is also a package deal now—you pay to have a leader, sag wagon, food and lodgings! These can be easy on the pocketbook and nerves, for most of the snags have been worked out. No worrying about running out of cash, or not finding lodgings at night. The routes are designed for comfortable riding, with most days 40-60 miles. Sightseeing and casual biking are the main considerations here. Trips take place is all parts of the world. For more information about this type of tour contact the following:

American Youth Hostels, Inc.
National Campus
Delaplane, Virginia   22025

Bicycle Touring League of America
c/o Dr. Roland C. Geist
260 West 260th Street
New York, New York   10471

Bike Dream Tours, Inc.
P. O. Box 20653
Houston, Texas   77025

International Bicycle Touring Society
846 Prospect Street
La Jolla, California   92037

League of American Wheelmen
19 South Bothwell
Palatine, Illinois   60067

Centennials are another popular tour. These 100-mile routes often become races for some. Generally they are conducted over a course to be completed in 12 hours or less. Sag wagons accompany the group. These are usually open invitational tours sponsored by a bike club.

Other tours are designed to be very short fun outings using themes such as progressive dinners, treasure hunts, early morning runs to a camp-out breakfast, and similar good times events.

Touring books of interest include the following which are nationwide in coverage.

Bicentennial Bike Tours, describes in a general way 200 tours that include visits to historical sites. Maps and photos.

North American Bike Atlas, Warren Asa, describes in a general way 152 tours. Rough maps.

ON CHOOSING A TOURING BIKE

Bikes are very personal possessions, like gloves and shoes— and they better fit or else the wearer is miserable! Selecting the right size and type of vari-speed bike is most important. A 3-speed will do well on routes without grades and of short mileage. If it's to be easy touring a 5-speed can handle small hills. But if touring is to be on varied terrain over long mileages, with good speeds necessary, then a 10-speed offers the best features. Indeed, some sponsored and guided tours now require 10-speed bikes for all participants.

In covering the trails described in this book this writer used an American bike made by AMF Wheel Goods Division. Their *Roadmaster T-1720* model proved to be a reliable bike. It was given constant attention and all good maintenance practices were followed.

For detailed information about selecting a bike for touring check into some of the books listed at the end of this chapter.

EQUIPMENT FOR BIKE TOURING

Bicycle touring, especially overnight touring, usually requires the use of bags to carry personal items or camping gear. For those who plan to spend their nights indoors, and take their food in restaurants, there is litttle more to carry other than personal items, raingear and repair equipment for their bike. If it is to be a camping tour then bikers will want adequate gear for sleeping and cooking out. A popular alternative is to combine both ways, such as eating meals out while camping at night. A small stove still comes in handy for an early morning cup of coffee in camp, or a late night snack at fireside.

Bicycle bags such as those made by *Hubbard* are excellent help-mates, spacious enough to carry everything a biker might need. A variety of sizes and styles are available, with large panniers fitting over rear wheel and doing the major job of housing gear. Front wheel panniers are favored by some. Other bags fit on the handlebars and seat. Some bikers use small backpacks, but steer clear of any large packs that will disturb your balance and riding efficiency.

How-to bicycle books and magazine articles furnish gear lists for touring, along with lots of tips for outfitting and carrying off a tour successfully. *Bike Tripping* by Tom Cuthbertson, *Two Wheel Travel* by Peter Tobey, and *Freewheeling: The Bicycle Camping Book* by Raymond Bridge are fine reference books for those getting into bike touring.

TRANSPORTATION FOR BIKES

Trains, buses and airlines are now providing service that will get the bike there for you, and usually at the same time. For the few who travel by train there is the baggage car for their bikes. This is inexpensive transportation. However, railroads have their way of doing things so check with ticket agents before traveling. Folding bikes usually can go aboard with commuters or long distance travelers.

Greyhound and Trailways will ship a bike to any of their terminals handling package express. They will hold it free of charge for 3 days, then 25 cents a day after that. Bikes must be in a carton. Maximum length in state is 84″. Maximum length out of state is 60″. However, remember that while the trip to the start has been solved the return trip is something else, especially if the last leg of a tour ends at a point distant from the start; the carton is gone and there might not be one available, even if there is a bike shop in the area. A possible solution is to send the empty carton ahead to a bus terminal, pay the nominal charges and have it waiting for your arrival.

Airlines are very accommodating now, but they also have their procedures. Check with the one you will travel. While some airlines do not require a packaged bike, others want the bike in a

carton provided by you or them. They have package size re-
strictions just like the bus companies. Be assured that while
every airline must carry your bicycle today, the smaller ones
may send it by another flight due to limited baggage space.

SAFETY

Riding a bicycle safely should be foremost in every biker's mind.
To a large extent his safety depends on him alone. Most of us,
besides being bikers, are motorists. And most of us are aware
that all too many bikers, like motorists, commonly violate traffic
rules and good driving practices. Keep in mind that *motorists do
not see bikes!* They are looking for cars—not bikes, motorcycles
and pedestrians. Educate other bikers, especially those who evi-
dently believe they are going to live forever.

Remember there are no special rules for bikers. Ride on the
right side with traffic. Ride single file and use hand signals.
Obey all traffic signals and yield to cars and pedestrians. Get off
the road and dismount when highway traveling with passing
trucks; they can blow you off the road. And remember that a
motorist speeding at 60 mph does not want to slow down for a
20 mph biker. He resents your slowness, especially if you re-
fuse to keep to the side of the road. Keep an ear open for coming
traffic noises and use a mirror. Bike flags and safety color clothing
are worthwhile investments. *And keep off the roads at night:*
elaborate reflection and lights are seldom recognized by speeding
motorists.

THE NEED FILLED BY THIS BOOK

A number of excellent guides are being published to cover bike
trails and tours in different states. Most of these are local in
nature and some of them are noted in this text. However, there is
a need for a book that covers in detail bike trails from different
parts of our nation. This book fills that need as a guide to selected
trails in an easy-to-consult format.

Beginners and experienced alike will find in these pages tours
that suit their skills and preferences. The text will help familiarize the biker with the trail and the area they plan to tour. Detail
information will include places to eat, sleep, buy food, launder
clothes, to see historical and scenic sites, to fix a bike, to find
recreation and many other things of interest to bike tourers. Al-

though this book can be used without further reference, other maps, guides and reading matter will make any trip better. These are included with names, addresses and prices.

HOW TRAILS WERE CHOSEN FOR THIS BOOK

Forty-five tours are described here in detail, along with mention of other possibilities. Cities with bikeways are also covered. Choosing tours for inclusion was not an easy task. Certain criteria was followed in order to come up with good trails. Scenic value, length of tour, type of terrain, traffic conditions, points of interest and accommodations were given prime considerations. Variety was also important, trails being selected in different parts of a

Grand Tetons from Jackson Hole.

state where this was feasible. Certain areas such as prairies, deserts, canyons and extremely difficult mountain routes are not covered because they proved too windy, hot or difficult for comfortable biking. Borderline cases include a suggestion that they be biked in cooler weather or by a very hardy biker.

Another consideration has been the biking family or small group. Most of these trails are suitable for experienced youngsters who are riding a 10-speed bike. Two thirds of these trips are loop tours, minimizing transportation problems for traveling bikers. The one-way tours generally start and finish at a point with transportation services: air, bus or rail.

HOW TRAILS WERE RATED FOR THIS BOOK

There is no accepted rating system for bike tours. Certainly the terrain is the single most important factor in rating any trail. Traffic and road conditions must also be considered. Even the weather, if it is unusually bad, should have a bearing on trail ratings; strong prevailing winds will make any ride an effort, whereas tail winds smooth out a lot of miles for a biker. Each trail described in this book will include a rating determined by terrain, mileage and traffic, road conditions, etc.

Tours selected are generally 40-60 mile days, easily maintained by most bikers. Riding at an average 8-10 mph for 6 hours a day will accomplish 40-60 miles a day with plenty of time for eating, resting, and sightseeing. Some trips included here are of short mileage, but with lengthy stays at points of interest, making for a full day of recreation.

HOW TO USE THIS BOOK

In the text several recurring headings are used to familiarize the reader with the trails described and to help him, within the scope of this book, to decide on a trip. These headings and the information they encompass are as follows:

Location   Geographic location of tour.

Season   Best time for biking.

Transportation   Services to start and finish.

Rating   Terrain, road condition, traffic, etc.

Reference   Other guides, maps and information.

Tour Outline   Mileages, time, accommodations, camping, stores, points of interest, bike shops, etc. The designation *full* *services* includes at least food, lodgings, store and laundromat. Laundromat is mentioned for those wet days. Stores are used as the main mileage check points, besides route changes, because they generally provide food, drink and telephone. Many are associated with gas stations. Accommodations are only named and described when they are the suggested overnight stop.

The inclusion of all known food, lodgings and campground facilities will allow a tourer to vary trips as to length of day. Or bikers can use just a part of these outlines as a leg of another tour.

The routes generally go through towns, rather than around them, providing the biker access to services. It's easier to get lost in suburbia and the dogs are very big!

All mileages indicated are approximate, given the vagaries of equipment and the operator.

A diagrammatic map will show the route. However, there is no reason why it must be adhered to strictly. Be flexible and imaginative. Know your limits and desires, and do not hesitate to take side trips. Or add an extra day and stretch the tour to include some fishing or a short hike. For hardy bikers some of these trips outlined as 2-day tours can easily be done in one. Often the suggested overnight stops are for campers only, or motelers only. Other tours suggest a use of both accommodations. However, by tailoring your daily mileage you can have whatever you want.

REFERENCE MATTER

It is intended that this book not only be a guide for bike tourers, but also a reference in matters of interest to bikers. Included in the following are lists of bicycle organizations, books and magazines, and information about maps that will be of service to the reader.

Organizations

Many clubs and groups in our country are devoted to furthering biking as a recreation and a sport. At present several organizations function on a national level. They sponsor and conduct local, national and international events for biking enthusiasts. Their periodicals keep bikers abreast of current news about their sport. And they continue to be the best means of maintaining communication between people who are likeminded in their appreciation of the values gained from biking. Some of them are listed below.

American Youth Hostels, Inc.
National Campus
Delaplane, Virginia   22025

Bicycle Institute of America
122 East 42nd Street
New York, New York   10017

Bicycle Touring League of America
c/o Dr. Roland C. Geist
260 West 260th Street
New York, New York   10471

Bike Dream Tours, Inc.
P. O. Box 20653
Houston, Texas   77025

International Bicycle Touring Society
846 Prospect Street
La Jolla, California   92037

League of American Wheelmen
19 South Bothwell
Palatine, Illinois   60067

Affiliated with these national organizations are local clubs. Membership in one of these smaller groups is the best way to become involved in bike touring. Many clubs conduct local and statewide tours. All of them are made up of people eager to assist new members. Contact one of these clubs nearest you through the above addresses. Your membership will add strength to the biking fraternity and enrich your own life.

Books
Many volumes have been written about how to choose, ride and maintain a bicycle. Included here is a partial list. Some of these names can be found in libraries. Others are advertised in magazines and organization periodicals. Outdoor recreation equipment

suppliers' catalogs usually list some bike books; many have sections of their catalogs set aside for biking gear. In the text reference is made to other books along with prices and sources.

Every biker will be interested in BOOKS ABOUT BICYCLING, P. O. Box 208, Nevada City, California 95959. Send for their catalog. It is the most complete list available in one place.

ANYBODY'S BIKE BOOK by Tom Cuthbertson
BIKES by Stephen C. Henkel
BIKE TRIPPING by Tom Cuthbertson
THE BICYCLE, A GUIDE AND MANUAL by
    R. John Wray
THE COMPLETE BOOK OF BICYCLING by
    Eugene A. Sloane
FIX YOUR BICYCLE by Eric Jorgenson and Joe Bergman

For a complete Bicycle Bibliography see the 1973 July and August issues of *BICYCLING!*

Publications

On the newsstands and through subscriptions several publications are available. These magazines feature articles on touring, product evaluation, new equipment and general information of interest to the biker. Good reading for the beginner and experienced.

BICYCLING!
P. O. Box 3330
San Rafael, California   94901

THE BICYCLE PAPER
P. O. Box 842
Seattle, Washington   98111

BICYCLE SPOKESMAN
19 South Bothwell
Palatine, Illinois   60067

BIKEWAYS NEWSLETTER
Bicycle Institute of America
122 East 42nd Street
New York, New York   10017

BIKE WORLD
P. O. Box 366
Mountain View, California 94040

Maps and Guides
Road maps are the most general maps to use for biking routes. They are adequate when used with other reading matter easily obtained from local and state travel commissions. Caution: use road maps published by the various oil companies rather than official state maps that come from travel commissions. These are notoriously inadequate when it comes to showing existing roads. County maps on a larger scale can be used effectively in planning short tours and looping routes, especially when trying to remain on little traveled roads. When biking in mountainous regions consider those maps produced by the U. S. Geological Survey. Of interest to the biker are the 15 minute quadrangle series. The 7½ minute series cover too small an area. Planning a tour with these maps will give an accurate picture of elevation gains. Index sheets showing the names and locations of these quadrangles in states west of the Mississippi can be had free of charge by writing:
Distribution Section
Geological Survey
Federal Center
Denver, Colorado 80225
For index sheets and maps of areas east of the Mississippi write:
Distribution Section
Geological Survey
1200 South Eads Street
Arlington, Virginia 22202
When ordering a quadrangle map be sure to specify name, series and state in which it is located. List maps alphabetically. Enclose 75 cents for each map.
Some U. S. Forest Service maps are excellent guides, complete with elevations and descriptive matter of interest.

CHAPTER 2

TRAILS SOUTH

THE TOURS DESCRIBED in this region are generally east and south of the Mississippi-Ohio Rivers. Topographically this is a region of rolling hills and flat country once away from Appalachia. Bikers enjoy a long season in the South, and it's year-round biking in the Gulf Coast states on an abundance of good roads that do not suffer the ravages of winter snow and ice.

Predominantly rural countryside allows a biker to get out on roads that see few cars. Chances for wildlife sightings are good and scenic pollution away from towns is at a minimum. There is a choice of mountain touring in the Carolinas and Virginias, bayou touring in Louisiana, tidewater routes along the Georgia coast and beach cycling in Florida. It all adds up to a real fun region for the biker.

FLORIDA

It's biking year-round in Florida, with more reliable good weather than anywhere else in the nation. While much of our country is

Fort Clinch.

suffering through snow and cold, Florida bikers are touring in
sunshine and comfortable weather. Summer biking is best on the
coast routes where cool breezes and temperatures under 90 are
common.

It is hard to find better roads for biking in our nation. Not
only are the surfaces good, but the traffic is light and the scenic
pollution is at a minimum. Tough hills are few and a biker in
Florida finds the miles passing easily.

The Tampa Bay area, Orlando, Jacksonville and Miami offer
the attraction of big cities, while northern and central Florida is
a region of rolling hills, lakes, forests and orange groves with
sleepy towns and their shady lanes, tin-roof homes and country
stores. Much of the state's east and west coasts are resort beach
areas with roads and services at the water's edge.

The state of Florida is very active in developing bicycle
safety trails. Currently funded is the first 13 miles of a trail that
will one day run 250 miles from Hobe Sound southwest to Key
West alongside the overseas highway. This is sure to be one of
the best and most scenic routes in America.

A signed 100-mile route now leads bikers over quiet secondary roads in very scenic country from Tampa southeast to Sebring.

The state has also designated bike trails in its park system. Routes range from a couple of miles to 30 miles. Most of these parks have bike rentals.

While the state has been providing routes for bikers, so have the cities of Florida. While most city routes are no more than designated roads some of these systems are quite good.

Homestead in metropolitan Dade County is where the concept of bicycle safety trails originated when in 1961 that 25-mile bikeway was started. Since then many miles have been added to make up a 100-mile system of well-marked roadways for safe and scenic biking.

The League of American Wheelman hold their Winter Rendezvous here in early March. A week of biking takes people on tours, among other places, to the Atlantic, the Keys and the Everglades National Park.

Tallahassee has developed a Bike-Route System that includes 50 miles of scenic, recreational and commuting routes. As the state capitol and a university town, Tallahassee has done an excellent job of routing the bike trails through scenic parts of town.

Those interested in longer touring can bike west of the city into the Appalachicola National Forest with its forest and streams, campsites and lightly traveled roads.

For more information and a map write to the Tallahassee Recreational Department, City Hall, Tallahassee, Florida 32304. Include a stamped, self-addressed envelope.

Visitors to Florida can obtain more information about the state from the Department of Natural Resources, Larson Building, Tallahassee, Florida 32304.

TOUR 1

Riding north from Tampa bikers will get a good feeling for the ridge country of central Florida as they head towards Ocala National Forest. This is a very scenic route in a mostly rural setting, biking on winding narrow roads amongst beautiful oaks, lakes and rolling hills, orange groves, farms and open grazing lands. In spring and summer the roadsides are lined with wildflowers.

In the fall there are enough hardwoods to bring color to the woods.

This is a camping tour with overnights spent at waterside. If time permits the 3 days can be extended easily by taking a day off to canoe the Withlacoochee River at Camper's World or the cold spring creek out of Juniper Springs where canoe rentals are available.

Location   Central Florida.

Season   Year-round; November thru April is best.

Transportation   Bus, AMTRAK, airlines to Tampa. Bus and airlines to Ocala, about 30 miles west of Juniper Springs at end of tour.

Rating   The terrain is mixed: flat at first, then becoming very hilly by the end of the first day. Mostly level on second day. More hills on third day. Road conditions are generally very good: light traffic and good paving. This is a moderate camping tour in a mostly rural setting.

Reference   Map-brochure of Ocala National Forest. Write District Ranger, Lake George Ranger District, Ocala, Florida 32670.

Tour Outline   150 miles, one way: 3 days, 2 nights.

Tampa is a large metropolitan area with full services and all the amenities large cities can offer: good eating, theatres, museums, libraries, etc. Of interest to visitors is Spanish Tampa, Ybor City, with its narrow streets and cigar industry. The very popular Gasparilla is held in February, celebrating the state fair days. It features a parade and the "conquering" of the city by a band of ruthless pirates complete with costumes and pirate gunboat.

    0.0 Exit from Tampa International Airport to take State
         60/589 west. Paved shoulders with heavy traffic. The
         setting is flat and open as you skirt airport grounds.
    1.4 State 60 goes left. Keep north on State 589.
    2.6 Red light. Gas station, then convenience store.
    3.2 Right on State 580.
    5.0 Small shopping center, then a large one: food, bakery,
         laundromat, department store, etc. Traffic remains heavy.
    5.8 Left on State 597: 4 lanes. Heavy traffic. Industrial area
         with many shops and services.
    8.6 Pass over State 587: about 5 miles east is Busch Gar-

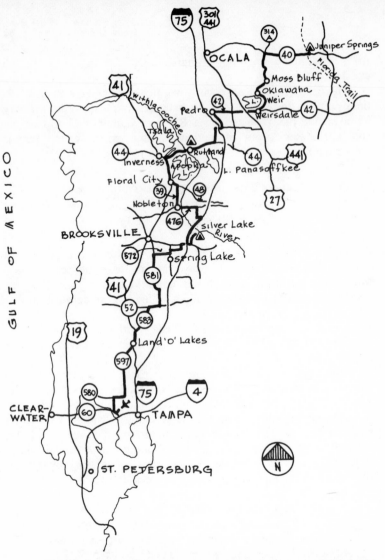

dens, a very famous attraction displaying animals from Africa, a monorail tour, beer hall, performing birds, etc. Another shopping center. Then highway becomes two lanes and narrow: not much room for you and a car. Traffic lessens.

11.9 Forest stand on right: cattle grazing under trees. Country now open and rural. Cypress stands, wildflowers.

16.3 Convenience store.

18.8 Left on US 41 north to Land-O-Lakes. Convenience store, bakery and cheese shop. Then a fishing farm.

20.0 Right on State 583. A narrow, good road winding among cypress and orange groves. Lakes and ponds. Some homes. Very light traffic. Wildflowers and song birds at roadside. Very scenic.

27.3 Right on State 52. Rough road. Shoulders can be ridden if light traffic or heavy trucks force you over.

29.2 Cypress Creek.

30.7 Left on State 581. Good, narrow road. Very light traffic. This is the hill country below Brooksville. Grazing land, beautiful lakes, ponds and great oaks streaming moss in the breezes. Mimosas blooming here in spring and summer are very lovely.

34.0 Triangle junction. State 578 goes right, keep left on State 581. There is a historical plaque here noting the Bradley Massacre of May 14, 1856 during the Third Seminole War, the last Indian uprising east of the Missisippi. The road beyond here is a rough one through scenic countryside; rolling hills, ridge views and nice shady rest spots at roadside.

36.3 Better paved road.

38.2 Enter Hernando County on another rough road. Tree types are changing to include more hardwoods. Good color in fall.

39.4 Cross State 420.

40.0 Camper's Holiday: camping, showers, store.

41.0 Sinkhole on left, then a rise to start the first long downhill run to meet State 572. Go right and up a rise to

42.5 State 581 goes left. Keep right on State 972. Hills in next few miles are very steep.

46.0 State 577 goes left. Keep ahead.

47.3 Left on US 51; store. This is the community of Spring Lake.

48.5 Right on Old Trilby Road, a beautiful lane under an oak canopy.

49.7 Old Trilby Road becomes a dirt road easily taken by a bike. Then pass White Road.

51.7 Left on paved Lockhart Road.

52.4 Right on State 50/US 98, then under I-75. Motels, gas

stations, restaurants. Continue on to just before R.R. overpass.

54.2 Left on Rital Croom Road, leading 3½ miles to Silver Lake Recreation Area. Road parallels and crosses railroad to

57.7 Silver Lake Recreation Area: camping, showers, swimming, fishing. Withlacoochee River.

0.0 *Second day* presents short mileage with a choice of directions. For the adventurous there can be a fence jump to get on I-75; take it just as you exit from the campground. Or head back 4½ miles the way you came to I-75.

4.4 Right on I-75. Signs prohibit bicycles. Ignore and take this to next exit, about 6 miles.

4.7 Pass over railroad and Croom Road. To the right is Silver Lake Recreation Area.

8.4 Pass over Withlacoochee River. A hike over the fence just before here will cut 8½ miles off the trip; it is only 2 miles from here to your next exit.

8.9 Interstate Rest Area. Toilets, water, picknicking.

10.1 Webster turnoff. Keep right and pass over I-75 on State 476B. Traffic very light. Open grazing lands, ponds, woods of mixed oaks, cypress and pine.

11.9 State prison.

13.5 Left on State 476. Traffic light, scattered homes.

15.4 State 575 goes north.

16.6 Cross Withlacoochee River and come into Nobleton: store, wayside park on river.

18.0 Right on State 39, a narrow, winding road with very light traffic.

19.0 Istachatta: fish camps, stores. Then enter Citrus County and cross railroad 3 times.

23.3 Junction. Keep right on State 39. Beautiful stretches with overhanging trees.

24.8 Left on State 48 into lake country, entering Floral City under a wonderful canopy of oaks. A pleasant town that has changed very little in the past 30 years: stores and cafe.

26.4 Right on US 41. Moderate traffic; heavy trucks. Scenery is dull.

30.6 Citrus County Fairgrounds. Upon nearing Inverness shops and motels in area.

32.3 Right on State 44. Inverness is left. State 44 passes along shore of Tsala Apopka Lake. Very scenic route. Wayside park one-half mile from US 41. Traffic is light; heavy trucks.

35.5 Convenience store; fresh vegetables. State 470 goes north here. The area is again rural, grazing, swamps and lakes in oaks and cypress woods.

37.4 Bicycle repair shop left, then riverside cabins. Campground off to right.

40.0 Cross Withlacoochee River. On the right ahead is Camper's World: camping amongst shady oaks, showers, laundromat, swimming, groceries, canoe rental. Recreation room. An extra day can be spent here. Rent a canoe and explore upstream on the Withlacoochee River. Remote, wild scenes.

0.0 *Third day* leave the campground and head east on State 44.

1.3 State 470 goes south to Lake Panasoffkee.

4.9 Left on State 475. Light traffic. Rural and grazing land.

5.8 State 462 goes right.

8.5 Cross I-75 to go left on State 475 north paralleling I-75.

12.1 Enter Pedro. Right on State 42, a good road. Store here on corner.

13.0 Peach orchards: relatively new industry for Florida.

13.9 State 467 goes left.

16.6 Cross US 301.

19.6 Cross US 27/441.

23.2 Left on Alt. US 27/441. Weirsdale: stores. Hilly terrain and moderate traffic.

25.8 East Lake Weir.

26.4 Public boat ramp on left.

28.1 Oklawaha. Right on State 464. Gas station, restaurant. Very shady route under arching trees.

29.6 Camping on right.

31.9 Groceries and trailer park. Then Oklawaha River crossing; Moss Bluff lock and dam. Fish camps. Restaurants and taverns.

32.4   Left on State 314A and enter Ocala National Forest. Light traffic through forest setting.

35.3   Private airport on right.

39.7   Right on State 40; groceries, restaurants and hardware store. Moderate traffic. Heavier on weekends as people come to Ocala National Forest for recreation.

42.2   Convenience store, then general merchandise store.

42.8   Ice cream parlor on right. A treat would taste good about now!

43.2   Mill Dam Campground in Ocala National Forest. A very nice spot on a lake. Flush toilets, swimming. Rolling hills now.

46.8   Fire tower on right.

50.0   Juniper Springs Recreation Area. Camping: showers, laundromat, swimming, groceries. This is a delightful place of shady campsites, hiking trails in the forest, clear spring water for swimming, tubing and floating. Rent a canoe and stay another day! Or plan to spend a couple of days hiking the Florida Trail where it passes through the forest.

TOUR 2

A seaside route, cool breezes, sunshine and flat terrain make this one of the best tours in Florida. Add to these the many historical and scenic attractions and it becomes one of the best in America. You are never far from the ocean as you bike from Daytona Beach north to Fernandina Beach visiting the locations of reconstructed forts, the oldest town in the United States and interesting places like Marineland where the viewing of sea life in giant pools is an exciting experience.

This coast has been important in North American history. One of the very first areas settled, it was wrenched by war and turmoil from the mid-16th century to the Civil War. Spain, France and England alternately controlled it or lost it in a series of battles; and all of them battled the Indians who were here in the first place. All of these people have left their mark on this land as best seen in the very lovely St. Augustine.

Location   Extreme northeastern Florida coast.

Season   Year-round for those staying in motels; ocean breezes are good. October through April for bike camping.

Transportation   Airlines and buses reach Daytona Beach. From Fort Clinch State Park one must bike over 30 miles to Jacksonville via the Buccaneer Trail and State 105 along the St. John's River; airlines, buses, and AMTRAK to Jacksonville.

Rating   Traffic is generally light, the roads narrow but good, and the terrain mostly level. Only about a third of the trip is through isolated areas. This is an easy tour in a mostly suburban setting. However, this is compensated for by the presence of the sea, the many historic sites, the attractions of St. Augustine and Marineland.

Tour Outline   112 miles, one way: 3 days, 2 nights.
Daytona Beach is a popular resort town famous for its broad beaches, surf, springtime college gatherings, auto racing and good times in the sunshine. The city provides full services.

0.0   Exit airport to a right on US 92, a 4-lane road with heavy traffic. Motel to the left. All the services are available along here: stores, shopping centers. Sidewalks can be used if traffic is too heavy in this residential area.

1.2   A unique tower structure marks the entrance to a fashionable neighborhood.

2.6   Cross US 1 and head out onto the beach over the Halifax River: Intracoastal Waterway.

3.9   Cross State A1A and go down onto broad beaches of Daytona. From here there are two routes north. Either take the beach itself for however long you like (in some areas it may be difficult to get your bike through the packed sand) or pedal along Ocean Boulevard, a narrow road between State A1A and the beach. You will pass shops, amusement center and amphitheater. There is a tower from which you can see 30 miles. This is a colorful neighborhood. In time you will want to rejoin State A1A via one of the many beach access roads.

5.6   State A1A is four lanes and easy to bike. Honky-tonk of Daytona Beach is left behind as the area becomes residential.

8.2   Ormond Beach: full services. Road becomes two lanes and is rough. Heavy traffic in a residential area that soon becomes motels.

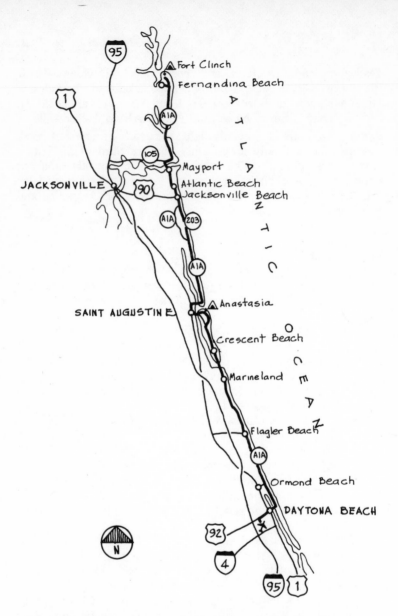

12.8 Road turns east and runs next to the ocean. Some services before route becomes more isolated.

18.0 Tomoka State Park 8 miles to left.

19.2 Flagler Beach, made up of second generation beach

houses built here in 1940's and 1950's. Very few services here. Some motels, but nothing big or fancy. A number of public shelters and turnoffs allow people to enjoy the ocean. Along this stretch the Intracoastal Waterway can be seen to the left. The ground cover is low and wind sculptured, the trees and bushes very dense.

20.0 Flagler Beach State Park. Camping on ocean shore. Restaurant nearby. Watch for osprey along this stretch, a large hawklike bird with dark back and light underparts. They hover above the water, spot fish and then plunge to capture it in their talons. A very exciting moment.

25.0 Beverly Beach and campgrounds on the beach side.

28.7 Road swings away from ocean to pass through an isolated area of oaks, pines and palmettos.

31.5 Shell novelty store. Ice cream store, then animal farm.

32.7 Interesting snoop and junk shop; perhaps a small souvenir piece of driftwood could be added to your pack.

33.0 Camping, convenience store, cafe, camping. Then it's back to the ocean shore again.

34.0 Campground on ocean.

34.2 Washington Oaks State Gardens; picnicking only.

36.4 Marineland of Florida, one of the finest attractions of its kind in the world. Services include food and lodgings. This unique sea life exhibit also has a marine research lab for the University of Florida. First-time visitors and those returning will want to spend a couple of hours here.

39.0 Matanzas Inlet. To the left and north is Fort Matanzas, a coquina rock tower built in 1740-42. Just north of the pass there is a museum and view wharf that looks across to the fort. Matanzas is Spanish for "slaughters". It was in this area that the then controlling Spanish defeated and butchered some 300 attacking Frenchmen led by Jean Ribaut, the Huguenot leader. Above Matanzas there are some fine beach homes as you approach Crescent Beach. Convenience store.

45.0 Frank E. Butler State Park; picnicking only.

46.3 Campgrounds.

47.0 Campgrounds.

50.0 Anastasia State Park; camping, showers. Or choose any of the motels in the area. Or bike into St. Augustine via route described below.

0.0 *Second day* continue north on Park road to spend the entire day in St. Augustine. Keep right at a fork in the road on Lew Boulevard. Ahead are lighthouse and water tower. Left at Carver Street to lighthouse. Right on Lighthouse Avenue. Left on White Street. Right on Magnolia Drive. Left on Ocean Way to State A1A. Right on State A1A.

2.3 Bicycle shop.

2.5 Cross bridge into St. Augustine, one of the most beautiful towns in America. Castillo de San Marcos on right. The city waterfront is very scenic, made up of old homes and green parks. The restored city, the old city and the new city all blend and reflect a common architecture. Narrow lanes and streets of cobblestone are lined with homes and shops, services, taverns, arts and crafts and small businesses. One of the best ways to see the city first is to follow a tour bus. Then go out on your own. Visits to the shops, the restored city, the fort and many other sights that will keep you here all day. At the end of the day return to Anastasia State Park or a hotel room.

0.0 *Third day* in St. Augustine go north on State A1A from campground to a

5.5 Right on State A1A leading east to the beach. The road here is narrow through a residential area. Traffic is light.

8.5 Campground.

9.5 Campgrounds. Above here the road is more deserted.

12.5 Residential area.

14.3 Wayside park.

19.4 Wayside park.

23.5 State A1A goes left. Keep right on State 203. Traffic is light.

27.6 State 210 goes left. Posh residential area of Ponte Vedra Beach.

29.8 Enter Duval County. Just above here take Duval Drive through residential area. Left on 37th Avenue. Right on 1st Street South to pass through Jacksonville Beach. Full services. Traffic is heavy. Two blocks west is the very busy State A1A with complete services and more room for biking.

34.5 Left on Atlantic Boulevard to State A1A. Keep right on road to Mayport Naval Station and Fernandina Beach.

38.1 Left on State A1A. Traffic is moderate through tide-water marshes and woods. Naval Station on right in distance.

41.3 Pass through Mayport to reach ferry at St. John's River. Nominal fee: operates every 30 minutes. Mayport is a fishing village with good eating places. Once across the river you travel north on the Buccaneer Trail passing the Huguenot Monument at Ft. George Inlet, Little Talbot Island State Park, Sawpit Creek and Nassau Sound to Amelia Island. This is very beautiful tidewater country. Welcome breezes on hot days. Traffic is light.

56.1 Store.

56.7 Right on State A1A and back to ocean. Very few services.

60.1 State 108 goes left, then come into Fernandina Beach.

62.0 Left on State A1A to Fort Clinch State Park. Camping, showers, store. Eight flags have flown over the fort since it was started in 1847 and discontinued in 1867. It has been restored by the Florida Park Service. Old Fernandina is nearby with its site of old Fort San Carlos. Full services in the City of Fernandina Beach.

From here the biker must return to Daytona Beach or go on to transportation services in Jacksonville; see *Transportation*.

GEORGIA

A state with forested mountains over 4,000 feet high, a piedmont that rolls down to coastal plains and a magnificent seashore, is bound to offer the biker exciting and interesting tours.

The mountains in the north of Georgia were once home to the Cherokee Indians. And it was here that America's first major gold rush took place. You can still pan for it. The rolling hills of the piedmont are the center of Georgia's commerce focused in the cities of Atlanta, Augusta, Columbus and Macon. To the south the coastal plains region includes the unspoiled Okefenokee Swamp, Savanah and the golden isles on the Atlantic Ocean. A long biking season, year-round in some areas, gives a biker a chance to see the state dressed for all seasons.

For information about vacationing in Georgia write the Department of Industry and Trade, Tourist Division, P.O. Box 38097, Atlanta, Georgia 30334.

Lunch stop in backcountry Georgia.

TOUR 3

The piedmont of western Georgia is a wonderful place to vacation. This loop tour north of Columbus includes ridge roads with matchless views of the countryside, the second home of President Roosevelt, a unique fun place called Callaway Gardens, and a glimpse of backcountry Georgia on roads where you will seldom be passed by a car.

Location   Western Georgia above Columbus.

Season   Year-round for food and lodgings. Spring and fall best for weather; summers are hot.

Transportation   Airlines and buses reach Columbus.

Rating   Traffic is generally light, except for short stretches and on the last day on US 27. Roads are narrow, but good except for the first day on Po'Biddy Road. Terrain is hilly, with some tough ones. The setting is mainly rural and pastoral with some isolated sections. This tour is moderate to difficult.

Tour Outline   151 miles, loop tour: 3 days, 2 nights.
The short mileage on the second and third days allows for visits

to the Little White House and Callaway Gardens. Columbus is called the "fountain city" because of the many fountains in public parks, at business and homes. The Confederate Naval Museum and the Fort Benning Infantry Museum will be of interest to many, as will a visit to the Columbus Museum of Arts and Crafts. Full services here in Columbus.

0.0   Airport exit. Right on West Britt David Road which becomes Miller Road in a half mile. Road is two lanes and narrow. Heavy traffic in this open country that soon becomes residential.

0.7   Keep right on Miller Road. On left is a shopping center: food store, laundromat, sports store. Restaurant on right.

1.6   Left on Warm Springs Road (State 1), a narrow two-lane road. Traffic is heavy in a suburban area, but lessens in a couple of miles. Many services along this route.

3.0   Learn the secrets of a dog house builder.

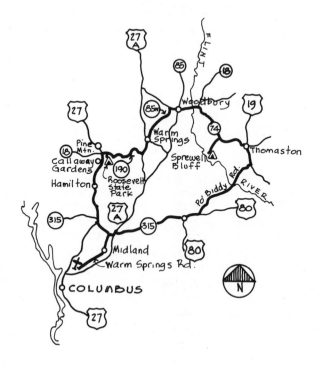

4.0 Flat Rock Park. A creek runs through this park, tumbling over great slabs of rock that provide natural water slides. Very popular with Columbus people. Picnicking and refreshments. Beyond here road gets hilly, treelined and scenic in portions.

7.7 Midland community. Rural scenery.

10.0 Natural gas company plant.

10.6 Right on State 315, then pass over railroad and come to US 27A. Take a left for a short distance, then right on State 315, a hilly, lightly traveled road through woods and farmlands. Good example of old southern farm houses now abandoned and in disrepair. First vistas of upper Piedmont.

23.3 Right on State 208, a narrow road with light traffic. Rough aggregate paving.

26.4 Talbotton: food, lodgings.

27.4 Left on US 41/State 80. Keep right on State 80. Traffic is light, but there are large trucks to contend with.

31.4 Left on Po'Biddy Road, a narrow, winding, hilly road through backcountry Georgia. These hills are going to tax the best biker; short, steep runs that will take some walking. Hazards are the sand from roads and drives spilling out onto highway. Paving is too rough for high-speed downhill runs.

37.0 Cemetery.

40.0 Cross Flint River. Paving beyond here is very rough as you climb to a ridge route with wonderful vistas of the Piedmont.

43.4 Rest stop with good views.

46.0 Left of US 19, a narrow highway with moderate traffic entering into Thomaston, a town with full services: bicycle shop. End of first day for those staying in motels. Campers will want to go on 14½ miles to Sprewell Bluff Park. In Thomaston, on Hannah Mill Road, visit the very beautiful gardens at Crystall Hills. About 10 miles south via US 19 on Allen Road there is one of Georgia's few remaining covered bridges.

48.4 Left on State 74, a windy, hilly road with moderate traffic. Mostly open farm lands here.

54.0 Food stores, then some good vistas.

54.5 Left at sign: Sprewell Bluff. This is South Old Alabama

Road leading 6 miles to the campsite. After about 3½ miles you enter Wildlife Refuge and climb to ridge road with spectacular vistas of the Flint River in its forested canyon. Tables and picnicking here. Hiking trails. Getting here is tough but worth it. Some hills to walk up and one big one down to Sprewell Bluff Park on the Flint River. Camping. No water or toilets. This is the end of the first day for hardy bikers: 60½ miles. All others stay in motels in Thomaston.

Second day via a challenging early morning ride return 6 miles to a

0.0 Left on State 74, still in rural country.

1.8 Public swimming pool. Fee.

3.0 Store.

5.5 Store.

7.0 Store and cafe.

7.5 Cross Elkins Creek.

8.3 Left on State 18.

9.5 Cross Flint River; restaurant.

12.0 Woodbury. Cross State 85. Stores, laundromat, cafe.

13.2 Left on State 85W: light traffic, wonderful vistas.

14.0 Lake Merriweather Recreation Park. Picnicking, swimming.

16.0 Store.

17.0 State 173 goes left.

21.0 Warm Springs with complete services. Cross US 27A and reach President Roosevelt's Little White House, a historical attraction that allows the public to visit the President's modest home away from home, now still very much as it was on the day he died in April, 1945. Food, gift shop, museum, rest rooms, picnic grounds and the famous unfinished portrait of the President. Fee.

25.2 Right on State 190, a winding, hilly road running over Pine Mountain and through Roosevelt State Park. Traffic is light. This is an exceptionally fine ridge ride through forests. Many good vistas, just pull your bike over to the side and walk through the trees.

30.0 Enter Roosevelt State Park.

33.4 Right on State 354 to the west.

33.8 Campground to the right.

34.6 Roosevelt State Park: camping, showers, swimming,

snackbar. This is the end of the second day for campers. Others can find lodgings at a motel just beyond the park entrance. Or continue on to Callaway Gardens or Pine Mountain for food and lodgings.

0.0 *Third day* continue west on State 354 to a
1.1 Left on US 27A to Callaway Gardens. Pine Mountain is one mile to the right with full services. US 27A is heavily traveled, especially on weekends.
3.0 Callaway Gardens offer complete food and lodgings. This is one of the most unique recreation facilities in America. Bikers will find many miles of scenic touring within the park: flower gardens, vegetable gardens, greenhouses, lakes and ponds, along with tennis courts, golf courses, water skiing, horseback riding, swimming, biking and fishing. Fee.
4.0 State 190 goes left. Callaway Gardens Country Store with light lunches. Vistas.
5.8 Motel.
7.8 Hamilton. State 116 goes left. Hamilton Square is a 19th century restored village on the square. Crafts, country store, eating places. Good place to while away an hour.
11.9 State 208 goes left, then a cafe.
15.3 Left on State 315. Just beyond here there is an open well on left.
19.4 Right on Warm Springs Road and return 10½ miles to Columbus and airport: 30 miles for the day.

MARYLAND

This is a biker's state. A good road system, plenty of services and accommodations, terrain that is easy on the legs and numerous points of interest add up to singular biking experiences within the state lines.

The western panhandle has hills to challenge the best bikers amongst forested mountain preserve, lakes and beautiful valleys. Northern and central Maryland are the historical areas where some of the great battles of the Civil War occurred. And before that the Revolutionary War hero Francis Scott Key wrote the Star Spangled Banner. Our nation's capitol is cut out of Maryland.

Maryland shoreline seems endless, wrapped around Chesapeake Bay and the Potomac River. Rich farmlands border the shore where small fishing towns offer the quiet and charm so readily enjoyed by bikers headed out and away from the bustle of cities like Baltimore and Washington. For the active sightseer a list of *musts* will include visits to Annapolis described by some as the "Athens of America", St. Michaels' Chesapeak Bay Maritime Museum on the Delmarva Peninsula; the Carroll County Farm Museum, south of Westminster; and in Baltimore it's the U.S. Navy's first ship, *Constellation,* and the B & O Transportation Museum in a railroad roundhouse.

Within the state there are developed trails for bicyclists. Some of them are listed below.

Annapolis provides wonderful bike tours into the past. Take a day and visit the State Capitol, the Naval Academy and the old homes where colonists and patriots once lived. Shady streets, brick paving, handsome architecture and charming gardens are all features of this tour outlined in the map-brochure *Historic Annapolis Bike Tour,* Maryland State Commission on Physical Fitness, 610 North Howard Street, 4th Floor, Baltimore, Maryland 21201. Free with SASE.

Baltimore County has designated a series of trails for bikers. They range from easy to difficult, 3 miles to 45 miles. The 12 tours lead through scenic countryside, rolling hill country, small villages and historic areas. For a map-brochure describing these routes write the above address.

C & O Canal Towpath biking is a singular experience. Stretching for over 180 miles up the Potomac River from Washington to Cumberland, the path is a hard packed dirt route about 8 feet wide. Much of it is a shady lane passing near towns like Seneca, Harper's Ferry, Antietam, Hancock and Paw Paw. Along its length campsites are spaced about every 5 miles; water and toilets. No cars here! The many towns allow for easy resupply. The Park Service recommends 20-25 miles a day for adult bikers. For a map-brochure and other information about the sections from Georgetown to Seneca write, Superintendent, George Washington Memorial Parkway, Turkey Run Park, McLean, Virginia 22101. For information about the section from Seneca to Cumberland write, Superintendent, Antietam C & O Canal National Park Service Group, Box 158, Sharpsburg, Maryland 21782.

Washington, D.C. has many miles of designated bike trails

including asphalt bike paths, sidewalks and side streets. The trails lead to all the historical and scenic points in the District. While these are mainly based on a daily-local basis it is possible to stay in Washington International Youth Hostel or a hotel and then see the city via signed bike routes. For information and a map-brochure of a *Bike Guide: Washington Area National Park* write, National Park Service, 19th and "C" Northwest, Washington, D.C. 20242.

For additional information about vacationing in Maryland write Maryland Division of Tourism, State Office Building, Annapolis, Maryland 21401.

TOUR 4

History leads us on this tour from Frederick into Gettysburg in Pennsylvania, passing sites of major events in Civil War history. These places have visitor centers, exhibits and tours to be taken. Connecting roads are scenic routes through the countryside and wooded hills. Harper's Ferry is a restored town that will interest everyone. A tour could easily include a longer visit here with a slower ride along the C & O Canal Towpath to camp at Antietam Creek before rejoining the road to Sharpsburg.

Location   Northern Maryland into Pennsylvania.

Season   Spring, summer and fall.

Transportation   Bus to Frederick and Gettysburg.

Rating   Light traffic, except on US 340 near Harpers Ferry and State 16 leading into Gettysburg. Roads are good except for the Harper's Ferry Road to Sharpsburg; this is also the most hilly of the first day. Another hilly road with dirt sections on start of second day. This is a moderate tour.

Reference   Gettysburg: Gettysburg Travel Council Information Center, Carlisle Street, Dept. 3B, Gettysburg, Pennsylvania 17325. Harper's Ferry: Superintendent, Harper's Ferry National Historic Park, Box 117, Harper's Ferry, West Virginia 25425.

Tour Outline   92 miles, one way: 2 days, 1 night.
Frederick is the site of the grave of Francis Scott Key, author of our national anthem. The restored home of the Union heroine, Barbara Fritchie, is here also along with Hessian barracks from Revolutionary times. Full services. Leave Frederick downtown on Jefferson Street which becomes US 15/340. Just before cross-

ing I-70 take State 180 to the right. This road parallels US 340 as you head south for Harper's Ferry.

0.0 Start tour at I-70 overpass. The road is a good one for biking: hilly, but with short rises. Asphalt and gravel shoulders. Traffic is light. The setting is rural with homes along the road. Vistas include ridges and manicured farmlands, small hamlets with church steeples thrusting up from the trees. In early summer the roadside is covered with honeysuckle and berry bushes in bloom.

2.0 Store.

2.3 Access to US 340; several of these along route. Traffic noises from US 340 are sometimes apparent.

4.6 Cafe.

5.0 Jefferson: motel and store.

4.3 Wayside Park: toilets.

6.8 Keep right on State 180 at this fork. Big run down after this. Cross a stream and climb up again.

8.0 Cross US 340.

9.7 State 79 goes left. Restaurant and gas station.

11.3 Cross State 17: motels and restaurant.

13.0 Knoxville: cafe and store. State 478 on left. Stay on State 180 then merge with US 340 for a while. Pass Appalachian Trail.

13.9 Appalachian Trail.

14.0 Take a right to Boonsboro, left over US 340, and back onto State 180. Take a right across railroad and head for Sandy Hook along side the railroad tracks on a rough, narrow country road.

16.0 Left for Sandy Hook. Pass AYH Hostel.

16.2 Just across the stone bridge, rather than going under the US 340 bridge into Sandy Hook, take a sharp right up to the Wayside Park on US 340. Cross the bridge over the Potomac and go on to Harper's Ferry. US 340 is a very busy road, but wide enough for biking. You go from Maryland to Virginia to West Virginia in a few minutes.

17.5 Appalachian Trail.

18.7 Cross over Shenandoah River.

21.4 Harper's Ferry National Historic Park. It was here that John Brown, the abolitionist, attempted to capture the Federal Armory some 17 months before the start of

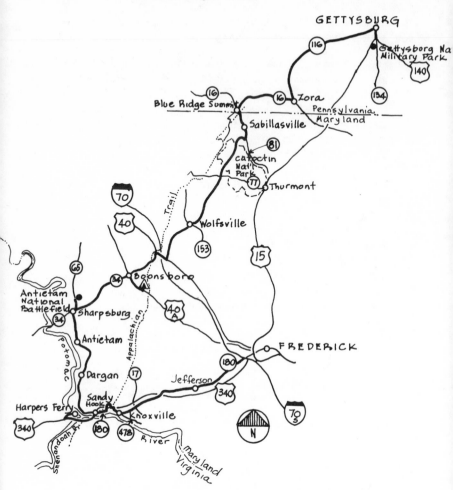

the Civil War. Harper's Ferry figured several times in that war and soon declined as an industrial center. Today many of the buildings still stand, one from 1775. Visitor Center, shops, exhibits, food and lodgings. Campground.

21.9 After visiting Harper's Ferry return along US 340 to cross the Potomac to a right at the Wayside Park and then down to Sandy Hook and the road to Antietam.

22.0 Sandy Hook. This is Harper's Ferry Road. Beyond here

to Sharpsburg it is a narrow, windy, rough, hilly road with some steep rises. Signs caution: travel at your own risk. Some walking here on steep rises. The C & O Canal Towpath parallels the road for a few miles. The towpath can be biked. This stretch of the river is a favorite take out point for many whitewater boaters on the Potomac. Good views of Harper's Ferry across the river.

24.8 Canal Campground on left. The land is wooded or farmed, scattered homes.

26.8 Keep left and follow signs: Antietam Battlefield. Pass through Dargan. Road remains very hilly as it passes over one ridge after another. Good vistas.

28.5 Store.

30.7 Pass large brick kilns now abandoned. Then cross Antietam Creek to pass through the town of Antietam. Store.

33.0 Antietam Battlefield signs on the way to Sharpsburg: food and lodgings here in Sharpsburg.

33.7 Right on State 34 then left on State 65 as you pass through Sharpsburg.

34.5 Antietam National Battlefield Site, scene of the bloodiest day in the tragic Civil War. Visitor Center. Rest rooms. Return to Sharpsburg and the end of the first day for those staying in motels or lodgings in Sharpsburg: 40 miles. Those camping go left on State 34, a wider road with easier grades than earlier. Beautiful countryside.

36.5 Cemetery, then cross Antietam Creek.

38.5 By-pass Keedysville.

39.8 Motel and restaurant.

43.5 Enter Boonsboro. Go right on US 40A to either of two campgrounds 4 miles east: Dahlgren Campground, showers; Washington Monument State Park. End of first day for campers: 51½ miles.

0.0 *Second day* bike the 4 miles back to State 34 and go

4.0 Right on St. Paul Street through the town swinging left to pick up the Boonsboro Road. The road is very hilly, winding and narrow, eventually becoming a dirt forest road that climbs over the ridge to US 40. It can be biked, but there is some walking.

5.5 Cleared area with good vistas. Then it becomes paved to a right on US 40, crossing I-70, passing Wayside Park and soon going

6.5 Left on Wolfsville Road, a narrow, winding, hilly road through the countryside. Light traffic.

7.5 Derelict steam engine tractor on left. Some good examples of old stone farm buildings in this stretch.

10.2 Cross State 153 and continue on the Stottlemeyer Road.

15.4 Cross State 77 and continue on Deerfield-Foxville Road, bear right, then left and follow the signs to the Owens Creek Campground in Catoctin Mountain Park. This is a scenic road that will bring you out to a

19.5 Left on State 81. Pass through Sabillasville to

21.7 Pass under railroad bridge and climb hill to Blue Ridge Summit. Residential area here.

23.0 Sign to Waynesboro. Go right and down the hill to cross the railroad tracks. Library here made from old railroad station.

23.5 Right on State 16. Restaurant, gas station. This is a wide 2-lane road with paved/gravel shoulders. Moderate traffic; heavy trucks.

26.0 Store.

29.0 Left on State 116. Just beyond here there is a small lake that is used for swimming and boating. Access at north end. Eating places along here, too.

31.8 Motel, and then the town of Fairfield. Stores.

35.0 Camping, store. Beyond here to Gettysburg the area becomes residential and commercial. Campgrounds, motels, stores. Enter Gettysburg and go

40.0 Right on US 140/15, following signs to the

41.0 Gettysburg National Military Park, the site where over 50,000 men were killed, wounded or missing in 3 days of civil war in July 1863, a year after the bloody day at Antietam. It was a defeat from which the South never recovered. You can bike over the battlefield. Visitor Center. In Gettysburg there are other attractions of interest to Civil War buffs. The town also has full services, bicycle shop and campgrounds.

NORTH CAROLINA

The Blue Ridge Mountains of western North Carolina are among the highest and most beautiful in the eastern United States. Atop these forested peaks a scenic highway leads from the Great Smoky Mountains north into Virginia. This is an excellent biker's route, albeit a strenuous one, that does ease off above the state line.

Away from the mountains bikers can head east across the piedmont through sleepy towns, orchards, tobacco and cotton fields to the coastal plains and the miles of resort beaches where roads lead to Cape Hatteras National Seashore.

Whether it's the mountain towns like Spruce Pine, the bustle and amenities of Charlotte, or the charm of college towns like Chapel Hill, in this state bikers will find plenty of reasons to visit North Carolina.

For more details on travel in this state write North Carolina Travel and Promotion Division, Department of Natural and Economic Resources, Raleigh, North Carolina 27611.

TOUR 5

Few places in America equal the scenic splendor of the Blue Ridge Parkway. Without a doubt this is our nation's most beau-

It's bike and hike on some of these hills.

tiful road. Limited access, speed and services make this a joy to bike. In the spring and early summer the mountain sides are painted with flame azalea, mountain laurel, berry blossoms and the profuse rhododendron. In the fall it's the show of October colors that bring bikers and hikers to this land. But most of all it's a quiet place where the signs of industry and commerce are absent. Even power lines are few. It's a memorable pleasure to pull your bike off the road and stroll through the forest, or find a secluded spot beyond the road and spend a half hour listening to the muted valley noises below, the insects, and the song of indigo buntings.

This tour includes the 3-day ride from Asheville southwest to Wesser where plans can be made to spend a couple of days canoeing, or hiking on the Appalachian Trail.

Location   Extreme western North Carolina.

Season • Spring or fall are best to beat the summer tourists in cars. But summer is extremely enjoyable at these Parkway altitudes and traffic is generally light.

Transportation   Bus and airlines to Asheville. Bus to Bryson City, about 15 miles north of Wesser.

Rating   This is a difficult tour covering the most mountainous section of this 575-mile ridge route. For the first two days the route is along the Blue Ridge Parkway where traffic is limited in numbers and speed. Road is excellent, allowing for fast downhill runs. The many tunnels will present a hazard. Reflection and lights are needed: enter the tunnels when you feel quite sure you will not be overtaken by a car. Third day of biking is on busy roads with a lot of short rise hills.

Reference   Write for map-brochure of *Blue Ridge Parkway,* Superintendent, P.O. Box 7606, Asheville, North Carolina 28807. Also ask for the booklet, *The Blue Ridge Parkway Accommodations and Services.*

Tour Outline   101 miles, one way: 3 days, 2 nights.
The short mileage on the first and third days allows for the stiff climb to Mt. Pisgah and time spent in Cherokee or at the Oconaluftee Visitor Center.

Asheville (2340) is an industrial and commercial city with a history of cultural contributions to the region including arts and crafts of its people, and the writings of Thomas Wolfe for whom

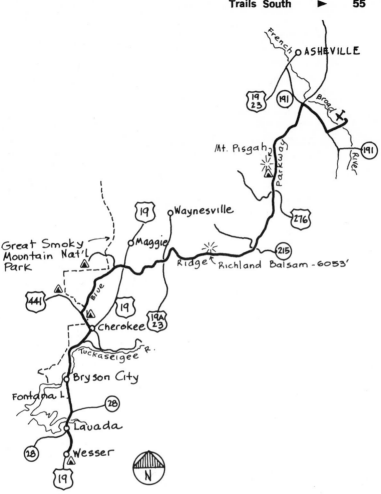

there is a memorial. As a mill town many fine bargains are available in the numerous factory outlets. Full services here, including bicycle shops.

0.0 Asheville Airport. Exit right and south on a narrow, winding County Road 1419. Moderate traffic. Rolling hills, farms and scattered homes. Blue Ridge Mountains to the right.
2.0 Cross French Broad River.

3.3 Right on State 191, a narrow road with light traffic.

5.8 Fresh vegetable stand, then community.

6.3 State 280 goes right, keep ahead. Store here.

7.5 Pottery shops, then road runs alongside French Broad River. A very scenic route with trees overhead.

8.6 Pass under Parkway bridge and turn onto Blue Ridge Parkway. Here you begin real mountain biking. The road is generally in excellent shape. Traffic is light and seldom doing more than 35/40 mph. Unlike the cars that are restricted to leaving the road at designated overlooks, bikers can get off at any time to view these wonderful vistas. The tour starts at about 2,300 feet and rises to about 5,000 feet in the next 14 miles with many ups and downs between. There are a number of tunnels.

22.2 Mt. Pisgah Parking: picnicking, comfort station.

23.0 Mt. Pisgah Lodge (5000) and Campground: store, restaurant and gift shop. This delightful place was once part of a 100,000-acre Vanderbilt estate where the nation's first forestry school was established.

Second day will include some very hard climbs, long and taxing. And the downhill runs are not the easiest. Lots of tunnels. The highest point on the Parkway (6053) is reached after 20 miles. An early morning start is recommended.

0.0 Mt. Pisgah Lodge.

1.0 Tunnel.

3.0 Wagon Wheel Gap. Cross over US 276 leading a few miles south to the Cradle of Forestry Exhibit in Pisgah National Forest. Beyond here are the first glimpses of the bald spots of Looking Glass Rock.

9.0 Overlook of East Fork Pigeon River. After this another overlook with drinking water.

13.6 Cross State 215 at Beech Gap.

21.2 Highest point in tour (6053). Then down to Balsam Gap (3370) and US 19A/23.

37.8 Overlook: drinking water.

40.0 Water Rock Knob Overlook: comfort station, drinking water.

43.6 Drinking water.

44.0 Soco Gap (4345) and US 19.

44.6 Drinking water.

46.5 Cut off to Balsam Mountain picnic-campground area and Heintoga Overlook, 7 miles. Campground open only in June, July and August. A one-way dirt road leads down from Balsam Mountain into Smoky Mountain National Park and the Cherokee Indian Reservation. This is a secluded and scenic alternate route to Cherokee if the Balsam Mountain Campground is used.

56.8 Terminate Parkway at US 441. A short trip to the right will bring you to the Oconaluftee Visitor Center with its interesting museum and restored farm buildings. Keep left into Cherokee with full services: campground, motels, restaurants and many tourist attractions. Be sure to include a trip to the Qualla Arts and Crafts Co-Op on US 441 just before turning onto US 19.

Third day mileage is short but this gives bikers a chance to see Cherokee or the Oconaluftee Visitor Center.

0.0 Junction US 19/441. Go right on US 19. Left is to Cherokee proper. US 19 is complete with services, but it is busy and narrow, with many short rise hills.

4.5 US 19A goes left.

6.5 Pass airport.

7.4 Cross Tuckaseigee River into Bryson City: full services.

14.6 State 28 comes in from left at Lauada. Keep ahead.

15.5 Cross over Little Tennessee River.

17.6 State 28 goes right. Go left on US 19.

18.3 Nantahala Village: complete resort.

21.8 Nantahala Outdoor Center in Wesser on the Nantahala River. Campground, motel, restaurant, food store. Center features outdoor equipment, horseback riding, rock climbing, canoeing and hiking. Outdoor arrangements can be made here to canoe flatwater in Fontana Lake or Class I-II whitewater on the Little Tennessee River. The more skilled can boat on the Nantahala. The re-routed Appalachian Trail comes through here and arrangements can be made at the Center to shuttle you to some point on the trail where you can hike back to the Center to your waiting bike. Equipment rentals available. For more information write Nantahala Outdoor Center, Star Route, Bryson City, North Carolina 28713.

Blue Ridge Parkway.

TOUR 6

No billboards. No power lines. No garish advertising. Limited traffic and limited speed. An excellent road. Bikers will find this section of the Blue Ridge Parkway the easiest, with many miles of gentle grades, ridge top routes to magnificent vistas, places of historic interest, good accommodations and biking conditions that make this tour a real pleasure ride through our pioneering past.

Along this road from Boone to Roanoke there are interesting places to visit. Many of them featuring crafts of the region as in the Brinegar Cabin. Restored buildings such as Mabry Mill are reminders of the pioneer past in these mountains. And the simple home of a legendary midwife is located alongside the Parkway.

Location   Northwestern North Carolina leading into Virginia.

Season   Spring, summer and fall. In spring and early summer blooming flowers are profuse. In the fall there is the color spectacle of the season's change.

Transportation   Bus to Boone. Bus and airlines to Roanoke.

Rating For the most part this road is between 2700 and 3200 feet. However there are some stiff climbs on the first day. Traffic is light and speed limited to 45 mph. Tunnels are the only hazard. This is a moderate tour.

Reference Write for map-brochure of *Blue Ridge Parkway*, Superintendent, P.O. Box 7606, Asheville, North Carolina 28807. Also ask for the booklet, *The Blue Ridge Parkway Accommodations and Services*.

Tour Outline 160 miles, one way: 3 days, 2 nights.

Boone (3333) is one of the most popular resort towns in North Carolina. It's playtime year-round here with facilities for all the outdoor pastimes, including downhill skiing and ski touring. In the summer months visitors come here for the cool temperatures, scenic splendor and many attractions. In June it's the spectacle of Wagon Trains moving along the Wilderness Road from Yadkin to Boone. This was the route used by thousands of settlers as they moved into the Middle West. An outdoor drama, Horn of the West, tells the story of Daniel Boone and the westward movement.

One hundred-mile views are yours from atop Grandfather Mountain where the visitor center features the largest native trout aquarium in the state and at lower altitudes a ride on "Tweetsie", a narrow gauge train, is a delightful experience. This train was once a working one, hauling passengers and freight into these mountains.

On US 321 between Boone and the Blue Ridge Parkway there is the Appalachian Outfitters who can arrange for canoe trips on the New River. Everything provided—food, equipment and guide. Sorry, no rentals without a guide. The New River is an ancient one, coursing north to Virginia and the Ohio River. Class I, shallow and swift. Good swimming. The setting is mostly pastoral.

If hiking the Appalachian Trail is of interest, the Appalachian Outfitters will store your bicycle safely, then shuttle you to the AT and have you hike a 2-3 day section south to north, then pick you up.

The center also features outings where you pan for gold or fish for trout or they will take you on a wildflower and bird watching trip.

Arrangements can also be made for you to pitch a tent on

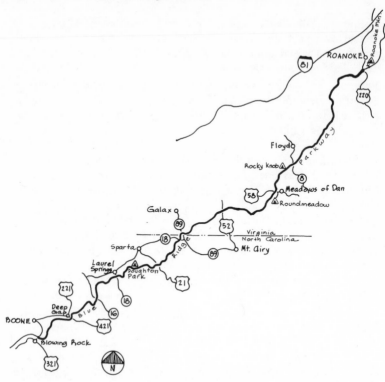

the premises. Count on all the assistance you need to insure you a good outing. For more information contact Appalachian Outfitters, P.O. Box 57, Boone, North Carolina 28607. Tel. (704) 295-3123.

0.0   Start tour south of Boone at junction of US 321 and Blue Ridge Parkway. Blowing Rock is just south of here with all the attractions and services of a resort town. Head north on the Parkway, a very stiff climb from 2,800 feet to 3,840 feet.

1.0   Green Hill Road goes right out onto a knob and residential area. Very scenic. The setting for much of this tour differs from the high mountains, dense forests and remote location of *Tour 5*. Here the roadway has fewer elevation changes, easier grades, more open scenery with many vistas to both east and west, and definitely a more pastoral feeling. Many farm roads join the Parkway, but traffic is very light.

3.0 Motel on right.
5.0 Bridge.
6.0 Road to Boone.
9.0 US 421 parallels Parkway.
10.0 State Rest Area on left on US 421. Then Parkway bears away from highway.
14.2 Cross over US 421 then climb to
16.2 Elevation 3,795 feet, and then more climbing.
18.0 Restored buildings.
18.5 Cascades Parking: comfort station and water.
22.2 Motel, store, restaurant.
28.5 Cross State 16.
31.0 Northwest Trading Post, a country store.
32.0 Camping on left.
32.6 Cherry Hill Coffee Shop: crafts, gas station.
37.0 Old log cabin on left beside road.
40.0 Bridge across Laurel Fork Creek.
40.8 Cross State 18. Laurel Springs is 2 miles to the left. Motels here for those who are not camping or do not want to push on to Doughton Park.
41.6 Camping on left. Very nice spot on hill.
43.3 Access to Ranger's offices on left.
47.4 Doughton Park: food and lodgings, store, gas station.
49.0 Campgrounds (3500): water and toilets.

Second day is easier as far as terrain goes. The road drops to below 3,000 feet and remains there.

0.0 Campgrounds.
1.0 Brinegar Cabin. Weaving and crafts. Very fine exhibits.
6.0 Stone Mountain Overlook. View of unusual stone formation much like a giant grey egg stuck in the forest.
8.7 Old mill pond.
9.2 Cross US 21. From here the road is quite flat for a while.
13.5 Cross Big Pine Creek.
20.5 Cumberland Knob picnic grounds: comfort station and water.
20.7 Cross State 18 again as it goes south to join State 89.
21.2 Enter Virginia.
22.0 State 89 overhead.

31.3 State 97: no access.

37.5 Fancy Gap: motels, gas station, store.

43.0 Orchard Gap: trading post, gas station, store.

46.5 Puckett Cabin, home of a pioneer woman who lived to be 102. As a midwife she delivered over a thousand babies, but none of her own 24 children lived beyond infancy.

47.4 Groundhog Mountain picnic grounds: comfort station, water, observation tower, fence exhibit. Small tower here for viewing: food and lodgings.

52.0 Cross State 779.

55.3 Country store on left.

58.0 US 58. Right to Meadows of Dan: motels, stores, restaurant. Camping here at Roundmeadow Campground, 1½ miles southwest on County Road 602: showers, store.

0.0 *Third day* get an early start so you can spend lots of time at Mabry Mill, the highlight of this day. More long downhill runs today with very few ascents that will be a problem.

1.3 Mabry Mill, one of the most photographed spots in America. A complete restoration showing how mountain industry included water powered mill, blacksmith, tanning, cane squeezing, etc. Restaurant, gift shop, rest rooms. Fresh ground meal is on sale at the mill.

3.2 Rocky Knob housekeeping cabins.

8.0 Picnic grounds: gas station, store.

9.8 Campgrounds: toilets and water.

11.6 Cross State 8.

17.3 Cross State 860.

20.0 Store and gas station.

21.6 Smart View picnic grounds (2500): comfort station, water, trail to one room cabin.

25.3 Store on right.

37.0 Sweet Annie Hollow.

39.2 US 221 left.

45.0 Bridge, then drinking water at Roanoke Valley Overlook Bridge.

46.0 Honeysuckle grows profusely along this stretch. Beautiful to see and great to smell!

50.0 Bridge: Back Creek. Then another bridge and a very stiff climb.

52.5 Parkway information booth.

52.7 US 220. Roanoke is left another 5 miles. Motels and restaurant to the right. Roanoke has full services: bicycle shops. Bus and airlines to Roanoke.

VIRGINIA

The United States had its beginning in Virginia when the first successful English Colony was established at Jamestown in 1607. For the next 300 years Virginia and its citizens were to figure prominently in our nation's development. Much of the physical evidence of this progress has been preserved or restored for our generation to view and reflect on in these times of hurried living and changing values.

The biker will find the backroads to history are a delight in Virginia. The scenic splendor of the Shenandoah and Blue Ridge Mountains, our first "western frontier", can be enjoyed for 300 miles from atop a marvelous Parkway. The many miles of sea-coast with its fishing villages, tidewater marshes, abundant bird-life and sprawling farms are all accessible to the biker on lightly traveled roads. And there are the historied cities of Richmond, Charlottesville, Fredricksburg, and Norfolk to visit. These places have been focal points in our sometimes turbulent history, yet they remain essentially "southern", their settings graced with an atmosphere of hospitality and charm. Biking in Virginia can be a very pleasant experience.

For tourist information write Virginia State Travel Service, 911 East Broad Street, Richmond, Virginia 23219.

TOUR 7

Central Virginia countryside is the setting for this tour from Lynchburg to Charlottesville. It includes a visit to the village of Appomattox Court House where the Civil War ended, and to Charlottesville and the house of one of this nation's greatest men, Thomas Jefferson. A visit to the University of Virginia is a must.

Location   Central Virginia.

Season   Spring, summer and fall.

Stop for gear rearranging.

Transportation Airlines and buses to Lynchburg and Charlottesville.

Rating Generally the roads are good, some high hills to climb at the start of the second and third days. Traffic is light other than first day on US 29 and State 60. This is an easy tour.

Tour Outline 114 miles, one way: 2½ days, 2 nights.
Short mileage days to allow for complete sightseeing at Appomattox and Charlottesville.

- 0.0 Exit Lynchburg Municipal Airport to a right on a narrow, hilly road through open fields; scattered homes. Traffic is light.
- 0.8 Right on US 29, a 4-lane boulevard. Heavy traffic with big trucks. Stores, motels and restaurants in the next few miles.
- 6.6 Left on State 24, a 2-lane road. Good road for biking; light traffic.
- 7.0 Store, then a right into hilly, rural country farms: woods and grazing lands. In some places trees close overhead. Vistas of nearby countryside.

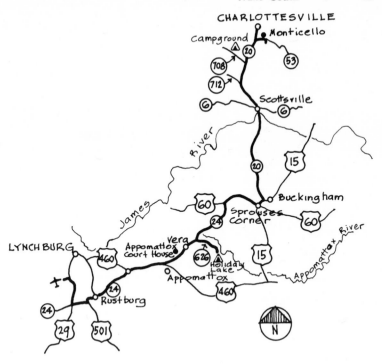

10.3 Cross railroad tracks, and go left on US 501. Sandwich place at the junction as you come into the town of Rustburg. Stay on State 24 and leave town on a narrow road.

17.0 Pass over railroad.

19.2 Concord.

20.2 Right on US 460, a 4-lane road with moderate traffic with heavy trucks. Store here.

27.3 Restaurant, motel.

27.8 Left on State 24; restaurants. Town of Appomattox to the right.

28.3 Left again on State 24. Campground on left, then a motel and restaurant. Soon reach the outskirts of Appomattox National Historical Park, site of the village of Appomattox Court House.

30.0 Entrance to the village where the Civil War came to an end on April 9, 1865. Fee. Consisting of several buildings, some of them restored, the town has many buildings open to the public. The house where Lee surrendered has been rebuilt. Self guiding tours. Water and rest rooms.

31.0 Appomattox River with a wayside rest area.

33.4 Gas station and snack bar. Then an antique store as you come into the town of Vera.

36.3 Right here on State 626 for 5½ miles to Holiday Lake State Park: camping, showers, swimming. Follow signs along a narrow hilly road through the woods. 42 miles for the day. For those who want motel accommodations there is the 17-mile ride to Sprouses Corner.

Second day it is 5½ miles back to State 24 and more of the same country: rolling hills, woods and good vistas over farmlands.

0.0 Right on State 24.

3.3 Service station, store.

10.2 State 24 ends. Right on US 60.

11.3 Store.

12.2 State 56 goes left.

12.7 Store.

13.6 Buckingham. From here to Sprouses Corner the scene is more rural than pastoral; scattered homes.

15.0 Store.

16.0 Motel.

17.5 Sprouses Corner. Left on US 15. Motels and restaurants here. (End of first day for motelers: 54 miles.)

18.2 Store.

18.9 Left on State 20, a narrow road with light traffic.

21.0 Store.

22.2 Store.

24.0 Store.

24.6 Cross Slate River, which you have crossed twice before as a creek; now it is larger. This stretch is more hilly. Some bike and hike possible here. Other parts of this road are secluded and shady; very pleasant.

28.8 Junction: store.

30.8 Store.

34.0 Store.

36.7 Cross James River and into Scottsville: full services. At this writing State 20 out of Scottsville is undergoing widening in sections. Heavy commuter travel in mornings and evenings, Scottsville to Charlottesville; other times the traffic is light. The route is very beautiful. Good vistas of large farms on nearby ridges.

37.7 State 6 goes left.

42.8 Junction of State 712; stores.

45.8 Cross bridge.

46.5 Left on State 708. Motelers bike on 8 miles to Charlottesville for full services: 37 miles for the day.

48.5 Campground, showers, laundromat, store, pool. For campers this has been a 54 mile day.

Third day on the road into Charlottesville is much like that from Scottsville; scenic, moderate traffic, good road with some steep hills. For those who went into Charlottesville for the night they will return to State 53 leading to Monticello.

0.0 Leave campground.

2.0 Left on State 20.

3.5 Store.

7.0 Store at intersection.

9.0 Right on State 53 to Monticello. This starts out wide and steep then becomes a winding, hilly road. From here you can look over Charlottesville. The setting is exceptionally beautiful. Fine homes and farms. Visit Michie Tavern, built in 1735. Museum and restaurant: fine food, 8 - 5. This colonial tavern was once host to our early patriots. Beyond is Monticello, the home of President Thomas Jefferson. This mountain top retreat was designed and built by the President. Tours, fee.

12.0 Right on County Road 795.

12.8 Ash Lawn, estate of President James Monroe. From here return 4 miles to a

16.4 Right on State 20.

17.5 Charlottesville: full services, bicycle shop. Charlottesville is a historic city, replete with its statues, tours of old homes, beautiful gardens and the first public university in America. Jefferson designed it and he, along with Monroe and Madison, were its first trustees. A walk through this aging campus can be an inspiring experience.

A wet stop on road to Yorktown.

TOUR 8

A visit to the sites of America's colonial beginnings and the end to our War of Independence are highlights of this 3-day loop tour out of Richmond. Plantations, historical sites, beautiful farmlands and small villages are all part of this run through Virginia's historical countryside.

Location   Southeast Virginia.

Season   Spring, summer and fall.

Transportation   Airlines, trains and buses to Richmond.

Rating   No hills here to consider. Roads are good and lightly traveled by autos, except around Williamsburg. Easy tour.

Reference   For maps and brochures of Richmond, Williamsburg, Yorktown and Jamestown write Virginia State Travel Service, 911 East Broad Street, Richmond, Virginia 23219.

Tour Outline   135 miles, loop tour: 3 days, 2 nights.
Short mileage days allow long visits in Williamsburg, Yorktown and Jamestown.

Richmond has been Virginia's capitol since 1779. It was

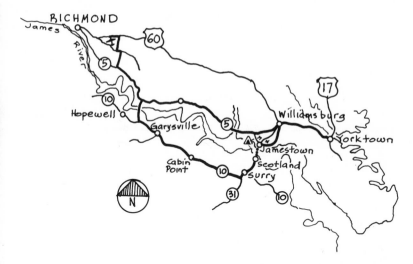

a seat of Revolutionary action and a center of commerce in a new nation. Largely rebuilt after its destruction the week before the end of the Civil War, it has grown to become a metropolitan area of one-half million people. Full services here. The airport is on the east side of town.

0.0 Exit Richmond airport. Right on Williamsburg Road, US 60. Motels and eating places in front of exit. Traffic is heavy on this road. You will pass through the towns of Sandston and Seven Pines, both offering services such as food and lodgings, laundromats, convenience stores, etc. The area is mostly a rural/suburban mix.

2.0 Right on Beulah Road; Nine Mile Road is left. This is an intersection with lights and gas stations. Beulah Road passes through a suburban area then into the country-side, skirting the airport.

2.7 Fire fighting school: model houses, airplanes, etc.

4.0 Cross railroad. Pleasant countryside.

5.0 Left on Charles City Road.

5.3 Right on Turner Avenue, a country road with light traffic.

7.0 Cross Darbytown Road.

8.6 Left on State 5, a good paved road with moderate traffic, some trucks. This scenic route parallels the James River, in a rural area. Some sections are wooded, while others are broad fields and farmlands. Trees overhang the route and occasional vistas appear on rises. While most people are speeding to Williamsburg via I-64 the biker can enjoy a pleasant ride on State 5.

9.7 State 156 comes in from left. Beyond here for a stretch the industrial pollution and stench from a paper mill is apparent.

17.4 State 156 goes right. This is your return route.

18.3 Convenience store.

19.0 National Fish Hatchery on left one half mile.

19.7 Berkeley Plantation entrance. Park and picnic grounds here.

22.0 Charles City: camping, stores.

26.6 Belair Country House, then a store and campground.

29.4 Sherwood Forests and President John Tyler's home.

32.8 Store.

35.0 Store.

38.4 Cross Chickahominy River. Campground beyond bridge: store, showers, laundromat.

42.7 State 614 goes right to Jamestown and ferry to Scotland.

44.5 Camping on left, then State 615; camping and stores. Beyond here, enter suburban Williamsburg.

46.8 Left on State 31, a four-lane road with moderate traffic. Pass William and Mary College Campus.

48.2 Williamsburg. Your destination here is the Information Center. Because bicycle traffic is not allowed through the tunnel of the Colonial Parkway, another route must be followed to the Information Center, rather than the one used when following the street signs. Go left on Boundary Street, right on Prince George, left to the Governor's Palace, and from behind it take the foot path over to the Information Center.

Williamsburg is the kind of place where people can easily spend a day or two visiting. It is a town of 18th century architecture, beautiful gardens, charming shops featuring outstanding collections of antiques, crafts and the work of skilled artisans. The best bet is a general admission ticket purchased at the Information Center. This gives you access to the shops, etc. on your stroll through the restored town.

Food and lodgings in town. Camping a few miles west and south on State 5 or State 31.

0.0 *Second day* start at the Information Center. Take the Colonial Parkway to Yorktown. This is a broad 3-lane road of rough aggregate concrete, center lane for passing. The traffic will be heavy during vacation months and on weekends. The route is very scenic and easy to bike. Many historical markers, some picinc areas.

5.0 Cross Kings Creek.

6.0 Felgates Creek. Road now is along the York River bank. Marshes to the right.

10.5 Cross State 238.

11.2 Cross US 17.

12.0 Cross State 238 to Visitor Center. This is the site of the decisive battle in the Revolutionary War when the British under Lord Cornwallis were defeated in October 1781 by the American and French under Washington. Nearby Yorktown, a prosperous town before the battle, never recovered. Food and lodgings in town, some of which has been preserved and restored. After a visit return to the 12 miles to Williamsburg and the Information Center. Keep ahead and ride under RR tracks and Lafayette Street to a right, then a left at the windmill on North England. Walk your bike across Market Square past the Courthouse, cross Duke of Gloucester Street, past the magazine and guardhouse, down South England Street and right on Newport Avenue to join Colonial Parkway to Jamestown.

24.0 This branch of the Parkway is just as beautiful as the Yorktown branch. Many historical sites along the way which is largely a water side route.

31.6 Junction. Ahead is Jamestown, site of the first permanent English settlement in America in 1607, 13 years before the Pilgrims landed at Plymouth in 1620. Only one structure stands today from that time, but remnants and diggings have revealed the town as it was once layed out. Visitors Center with exhibits and gift shop. Rest rooms. Return to junction and take in the sights of Jamestown Festival Park with a reconstructed fort and replicas of the three small ships that brought 105 men to America. Glass blowing, pottery, exhibits, restaurants, gift shop. Fee. Camping nearby on State 31, but no motels. End of the day for campers: about 35 miles. Motelers should return 8 miles to Williamsburg or go on to Surry, another 5 miles via ferry.

Third day take State 31 to the ferry, a twenty minute ride to

0.0   Scotland: store. State 31 traffic is light on a country road. The setting is rural with more vegetable farming here than on State 5.

5.0   Surry. Food and lodgings at Surry House.

6.2   Right on State 10, a good paved road with light traffic. Many historical markers along this Colonial Trail.

13.6   Spring Grove. State 40 goes left. Store.

14.5   Beautiful wayside park. Hills here.

17.3   Cabin Point. Store.

20.5   Burrowsville. Store. China shop; Prince George type.

21.7   Store.

26.0   Stores at Garrysville.

30.5   Right on State 156.

32.3   Cross James River.

34.3   Left on State 5 and return the 17½ miles to airport on route of first day. 52 miles.

TEXAS

As large as Texas is you would expect to find good routes for bike tours. And you will find them. While much of the state is too hot for biking during the summer, the weather and temperatures are ideal in spring and fall. In the winter tours can be planned for the Gulf Coast region, San Antonio and the hill country, and the far southwest Big Bend National Park.

The state has produced a series of 10 regional maps outlining routes to historic sites and scenic points of interest. They are designed to show off Texas to the motorist, but they can be an excellent reference and point of departure for creating bike tours. These maps are undoubtedly the finest effort of their kind in this country. For copies of these maps write Texas Highway Department, Travel and Information Division, Austin, Texas 78763.

TOUR 9

Biking through the forest country of east Texas is very pleasant touring. Rolling hills, lakes, forested roadsides and scenic farm country provides a wonderful background to a leisurely outing.

Historied towns like San Augustine were once stomping grounds for Sam Houston and Davy Crockett.

Location   Eastern Texas.

Season   Spring, fall and winter. July and August are too hot.

Transportation   Airlines and buses to Lufkin.

Rating   Generally good roads with light traffic in rolling hill country; some steep short-rise hills on second and third days. Heavy traffic leaving and returning to Lufkin. This is an easy tour.

Reference   Write for map-brochure, *Texas Forest Trail*, Texas Highway Department, Travel and Information Division, Austin, Texas 78763.

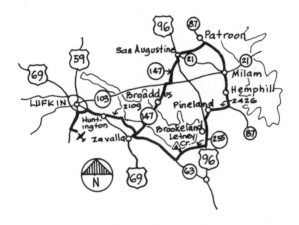

Tour Outline   190 miles, loop tour: 3 days, 2 nights.

Lufkin is a small logging town featuring the headquarters of the National Forests of Texas, a city zoo and a miniature railroad in one of its city parks. Full services here. The airport is on the south side of town.

0.0   Exit Lufkin County Airport on airport road through open country and woods.

0.6   Road comes in from right.

0.8   Right on US 59, a 4-lane road; poor biking shoulder. Traffic is moderate.

4.3   Angelina College.

5.3   Camping, then come into more residential area.

5.8   Right on State 287 Loop East: a 4-lane road with median and shoulder for biking. Traffic is moderate here. Full services at this intersection: motels, food, stores, etc.

7.0   Pass under Highway 58.

7.3   Right on US 69: 4-lane road with biking shoulder.

7.7   Cafe, then store.

9.0   Town is left behind as you move into countryside: farms, woods, scattered homes.

9.3   Store.

11.0   Junk shop. Large estates in this area.

11.5   Store. Highway 326 goes right.

12.0   Cafe.

12.2   Lufkin Tractor Company, makers of many of the semi-trailers seen on the highways.

14.0   Come into Huntington.

14.3   Highway 1475 goes left.

15.0   Left on Highway 1669 to Highway 2109 and pass through Huntington: cafe, store, laundromat here.

15.7   Right on Highway 2109, a narrow road with light traffic on this winding country route. Early morning smells include oak fires.

19.0   Baptist Church, then a more wooded ride as you near Sam Rayburn Reservoir. On a right bend: camping and store.

25.2   Highway 2801 goes left 3 miles to Hanks Creek Park on the reservoir: motel and restaurant at the reservoir.

27.3   Enter Angelina National Forest: tall pine forest.

29.0   Highway 3124 goes left to Monterey, then cross through an open area of sloughs and swamp: reservoir on left.

32.0   Right on State 147 for Zavalla: stores, cafe, laudromat. Then an immediate left on State 63, a 2-lane road with a wide biking shoulder that is not always passable. Traffic is light, but big trucks here. The area is open farmlands, woods and scattered homes.

34.7   Camping beside Angelina National Forest Zavalla Work Center.

36.5   Highway 2743 goes left 5 miles to Caney Creek Park on the Sam Rayburn Reservoir: camping.

38.4   Road to Bouton Lake: camping.

41.3   Store.

42.5   Road goes right 2 miles to Boykin Springs: camping. More hills beyond here on a rough road.

46.3 Road goes left 3 miles to Sandy Creek: camping.

50.0 Left on State 255: store.

50.3 Camping on left.

51.3 Road goes left 2 miles to Letney Creek: camping. End of day: 53 miles.

0.0 *Second day* return 2 miles to go

2.0 Left on State 255.

3.0 Sam Rayburn Reservoir.

4.2 Cross dam over Angelina River and the reservoir. There is a park here with water and toilets. Then cross over the earthern dam/causeway. Vistas. Hills from here to Pineland.

7.2 Camping: store.

7.7 Store.

8.2 Store, scattered resort homes in this area.

11.7 Left on US 96, a narrow 2-lane road with light traffic and big trucks.

15.4 Highway 1007 goes left; store.

16.7 State 149 goes left to Brookeland. Wide road now with biking shoulder. Scattered homes as you skirt the town.

17.5 Stores, camping, laundromat.

17.8 Camping, store. State 149 again goes left into Brookeland.

18.2 Enter Sabine National Forest.

20.0 Leave Sabine National Forest and skirt the eastern shore of the reservoir.

22.4 State 414 goes left.

23.7 Rest Area.

24.2 Right on Highway 1 for Pineland, passing through a pleasant residential area.

25.0 Right on Highway 2426. Pineland is ahead: store, cafe, laundromat. Road out of Pineland is rough and narrow in a forest setting. Easy biking.

28.2 Enter Moore Plantation Game Management Area. Very scenic ride.

31.0 Leave the plantation; short-rise hills beyond here.

33.7 Left on State 87, a wide 2-lane road with light traffic in countryside of farms and woods.

38.2 Enter Hemphill: narrow, rough road in a residential area.

38.7 Cafe. Motel on Highway 944 going right.

39.0 State 184 goes left in town: stores, cafe, laundromat.

41.2 More services: stores, cafes.

41.7 Leave Hemphill for wooded route on wide road through hilly country on easy grades.

45.6 State 21 goes left to Milam: store. Narrow road as you climb from intersection.

46.4 Top rise and then steep short-rise hills in very pleasant wooded country. Shady ride.

48.2 Road to Redhill Lake: camping.

48.7 Camping, cabins to the right.

51.0 Highway 276 goes right: store. Camping 2 miles down road.

56.0 Store.

60.4 Left on Highway 353 for San Augustine, a narrow road winding through farms and over short-rise hills as you take a ridge ride. Vistas here.

68.0 Water tower on left as you drop down into San Augustine. Full services here. San Augustine was known as the Cradle of Texas and its streets were familiar to many early patriots.

69.7 Left on State 147: store. Then right on State 21/147 to pass through town. The Cullen House was built in 1839; it's now a museum.

72.2 Town Square. Keep ahead on State 21 West. This is part of the Spanish *El Camino Real,* laid out in 1690 from St. Augustine, Florida to San Antonio to Mexico City to Vera Cruz.

73.0 Left on US 96: motel, restaurants. End of second day. Camping about 2 miles down US 96.

0.0 *Third day* head south on US 96, a busy 2-lane road with a biking shoulder. Nice vistas.

1.2 Camping on left.

1.4 Right on State 147 for Lufkin, a narrow, rough road with some short-rise hills.

7.2 Highway 1992 goes right: store.

8.2 Highway 705 goes left.

10.2 Right on State 103.

11.0 Left on State 147, a forested ride: scattered homes.

17.2 Highway 1277 goes right to Lufkin, then come into Broaddus: stores, cafe, motels. This is a resort area.

18.0 Highway 2558 goes left. Road out of Broaddus has more

motels, stores and cafes. Biking shoulder here.

18.4 Highway 83 goes left.

18.8 Motel.

21.6 Highway 2858 to Jackson Hill Park goes right.

22.7 Cross Sam Rayburn Reservoir on causeway.

23.7 Bridge.

25.2 Cafe, store: showers.

25.7 Highway 3123 goes right: store and motel. Some short-rise hills beyond here.

31.0 Right on Highway 2109. 32 miles to Lufkin Airport via the first day route. 63 miles for the day.

CHAPTER 3

TRAILS EAST

THIS IS OUR nation's most populated region, including those states east of Pennsylvania and north of the Mason and Dixon Line. Long tours in rural areas are hard to come by in the East. Nor is it easy to find routes that don't encounter some stiff hills along the way. While the frequency of towns make it hard to get into remote areas, they do provide points of convenient services and historic interest.

Bikers will find some remote touring in the Pine Barrens of New Jersey, or in upper New York and Maine where the terrain is often easy and the towns far apart. Mountain biking amongst the tall forest of the Adirondacks, the Green Mountains and White Mountains will challenge the very best bikers. For cool summer outings there are the ocean and lakeshore roads, often busy, but very scenic.

An excellent guide to touring in the east is *Northeast Bicycle Tours* by Tobey and Wolkenberg. This book describes in detail 130 tours in New York, Connecticut, Rhode Island, Massachusetts, Vermont, New Hampshire and Maine. Maps.

Coke break on Cape Cod.

MAINE

In New England Maine is a large state with a small population, and most of it in the southwestern part of the state and along the coast. The northern and eastern portions are, in many cases, remote wilderness, a land of vast distances, chains of lakes, mountains and quiet forests with few connecting roads.

The state has no program for bike trails, but it does encourage everyone to bike Maine's uncongested roads winding through their beautiful countryside. Especially scenic is Maine's rugged coastline with its countless islands and small villages.

Vacation planner brochures with travel information for Maine may be obtained from Maine Department of Economic Development, State Office Building, Augusta, Maine 04330.

TOUR 10

Lake country touring above Portland takes you on a pleasant 2-day loop outing. Overnight stay on a lake. Cool breezes, beautiful wildflowers and good views of the White Mountains as you bike on lightly traveled roads.

Location   Southern Maine.

Season   Spring, summer and fall. A swim in the lakes during late summer will be fun.

Transportation   Bus and airlines to Portland.

Rating   Unfortunately it is hard to find a good State paved road in Maine. Any stretch of good paving is always followed by a stretch of terrible paving—and so on! This tour is no exception. Traffic is light, other than on US 302. Hills are mostly short rises, but some are steep. There is a walk or two here, especially above Gorham. In early summer some of the paved shoulders have sand left on them from winter making them difficult to use. This is a moderate tour.

Tour Outline   91 miles, loop tour: 2 days, 1 night.
Portland is the commercial center of Maine and the state's largest city. Full services here; bicycle shops. The airport is on the southeast side of town.

    0.0 Exit airport via the north access road to take a

    0.8 Right on a 2-lane rough road. At first light make a left on State 22.

    1.6 Pass over I-95. Road passes through a mix of industrial and rural scenes. Then farmlands with scattered homes.

    4.8 Store.

    5.0 Rest Area. State 114 comes in from left. Road is now narrow and rough.

    5.8 Right on State 114 north. Good for biking, open and wooded countryside, scattered homes. In summer the fields are ablaze with colors; red, orange, white, blue, lilac—it goes on, just beautiful!

    8.6 Gorham: stores. Cross US 202. The road beyond here becomes hilly; steep short-rise hills with good vistas of

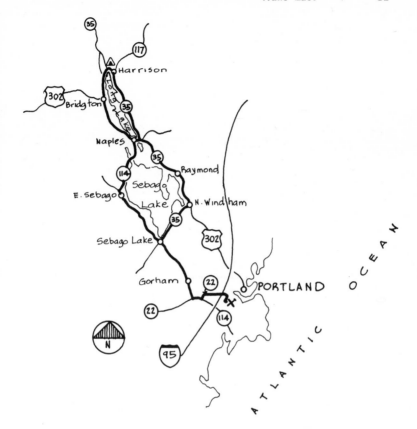

White Mountains in New Hampshire. As you come into Sebago Lake the area becomes more residential.

15.3   Sebago Lake. Cross State 35. Stores. The road skirts Sebago Lake to be seen occasionally. Road is wide and good for biking. Hills are easier.

16.6   Rest Area beside water: toilets.

19.0   Cross railroad tracks. Then come into East Sebago Lake: stores, cafes, cottages, etc. Boats for rent.

24.0   State 11 comes in from left: biking shoulder. Then it becomes a rough, narrow, winding road as you swing around north end of Sebago Lake. Lakeside homes. Traffic is light as you pass through wooded setting. Very pleasant.

29.2   Cross over bridge on finger of Sebago Lake.

31.0   Good road.

31.2   Sebago Lake State Park: camping.

31.6   Campground

32.0   Campground. Then come into Naples and go right on US 302. Naples is at the bottom of Long Lake. Nice waterfront. Boat rides on lake. Airplane rides. Food and lodgings. Stores.

33.3   Left on State 35. Motel and restaurant. Now on a narrow, rough road alongside the lake. Lakeside homes here. Some good vistas of White Mountains and snow patches on Presidential Range through early summer.

40.5   Start long downhill run to Harrison.

43.0   Motel on water.

43.8   Left on State 35/117 in Harrison. Stores, food and lodgings here: inquire. Campground also here on lake. End of first day: 44 miles.

0.0   *Second day* head south along west side of Long Lake. Good road with wide shoulders.

0.6   Housekeeping cottages and apartments.

1.1   Campground.

1.5   State 37 goes right.

2.3   Campground. Good vistas beyond here.

4.3   Bridgton. Straight ahead on US 302. Motels, stores, eating places, etc. US 303 is busy and narrow.

11.8   Rest Area as you come into Naples and pass through on US 302.

13.3   State 11 goes left. Restaurants and motels. Traffic from here on to North Windham is heavy. Road is wide enough for cars and bikes. Scenery is rather dull other than where you come close to the lake. Many commercial establishments.

15.3   Sebago Lake State Park.

19.8   State 121 goes left as you come into Raymond.

20.8   Rest Area next to lake; very nice.

24.8   North Windham: full services. Right on State 35, a narrow hilly road with moderate traffic through a shady setting of woods and farmlands. Scattered homes.

29.8   State 237 goes left. Vistas here across lake, north to White Mountains.

31.3 Sebago Lake. Left on State 114 south. Bike the remaining 15 miles to airport: 46½ miles.

TOUR 11

Spectacular scenery. Ocean views. Rocky coastlines and pounding seas. Fishing villages. Forest roads. Lobsters, clams and fresh fish. Maine arts and crafts. Great bald rock mountains dropping to the sea's edge. People have been living and visiting here since the days of the Vikings. And it's little wonder that so many have chosen to make it home. This loop tour south from Bangor is an exciting outing. The grandeur of Maine's coast cannot be seen better than at Acadia National Park.

Location   Eastern Maine seaboard.

Season   Spring, summer and fall. Always be prepared for inclement weather. Perhaps allow an extra day in your schedule.

Rating   Like so many of Maine's roads these, too, are a patchwork of good and bad. Some hills on all days, but generally short-rise. Traffic is heavy on US 1A and State 3 to Bar

Rugged Acadia coast.

Harbor. Around the villages and on the narrow roads congestion helps slow down cars. Easy to moderate tour.

Transportation   Airlines and buses to Bangor.
Reference   Write for map-brochure from the Superintendent, Acadia National Park, Bar Harbor, Maine 04609.

Tour Outline   135 miles, loop tour: 3 days, 2 nights.
Bangor is the eastern junction for all major roads leading into the remote north country and eastern lake region. From here there is no easy route to Acadia National Park; all the routes are busy. Bangor has full services; bicycle shops. The airport is on the northwest side of town.

0.0 Exit Bangor Airport and go right on State 222 (Union Street). Shopping center here; campground 4 miles left. State 222 is a busy 4-lane road with enough room for biking.

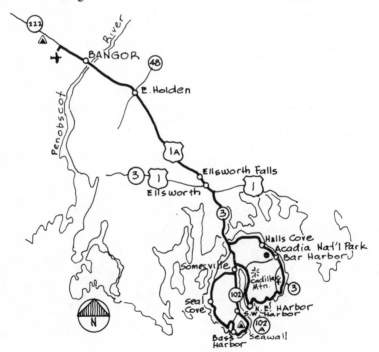

1.7   Cross I-95 onto a 2-lane road with room for biking. Leave the commercial behind and pass through a residential area.

2.6   Cross US 2. Services here.

3.0   Join US 1A and cross Penobscot River.

3.3   Cross State 15. Commercial area; busy road wide enough for biking. Setting is a mix of rural, woods and scattered homes in hilly country. From here on there will be occasional campgrounds, eating places, shops, motels, etc.

7.0   Road narrows.

10.8   State 46 comes in from right and then leaves left as you pass through East Holden.

14.0   Road is being widened. Good vistas beyond here of distant lakes and mountains. Mostly wooded.

23.0   Picnic area.

26.0   State 179/180 goes left as you come into Ellsworth Falls. Food and lodgings.

27.6   Join US 1/State 3 in Ellsworth. Full services here; bicycle shop.

28.6   US 1 goes left. Stay on State 3, a narrow road with a narrow shoulder.

32.0   State 204 goes left. Good vistas of mountains.

36.0   Cross the Mt. Desert Narrows onto Mt. Desert Island. Picnic area on left.

36.5   Campground. Left on State 3; State 102/198 goes right. Many motels, eating places and shops from here on. Good views now of water. Lobster and clams to eat here. The motels and cottages have very reasonable prices in June, competing with campgrounds.

38.0   Campground.

39.5   Campground.

41.5   Campground.

43.2   Hulls Cove.

43.8   Acadia National Park Visitor Center. Stop in here for map-brochure of island and latest information on weather.

45.0   Ferry to Nova Scotia.

46.0   State 233 goes right and come into Bar Harbor.

46.5   US 3 goes right on Main Street. End of first day. Go left and visit the shops and waterfront. Overnight in town or back at one of the many campgrounds.

0.0   *Second day* the road leaves town headed south between

the solid rock masses of Cadillac Mountain (1530) and
Champlain Mountain (1058) in a wooded setting.

1.3 Right on Ocean Drive, a one way loop tour to the shoreline and back. Hard climb up, but it is worth it.

3.0 Picnic area. You come out to overlook the ocean and out
islands. Spectacular views.

5.5 Sand Beach. You can drop down here for a swim in the
very cold Atlantic waters. This 2-lane one road has lots
of short-rise hills. You pass by the Thunder Hole and a
National Park Campground.

10.7 Pass under State 3.

11.7 Pass under another bridge.

12.0 Stables with horses for rent.

12.5 Left on State 3 to Seal Harbor, leaving the Ocean Drive
Loop. Two-way traffic on good narrow road through the
woods in a long downhill run beside a brook.

13.6 Right on State 3; Seal Harbor to left. Shoreline road
that becomes narrow and hilly. Big estates here; beautiful grounds and homes.

16.4 Left on State 198 for Northeast Harbor.

17.0 Harbor Drive leads down to Waterfront. Keep ahead into
town and take a right at

18.8 Sargent Drive sign: no campers, trucks, etc. Keep bearing right and bike on Millbrook Road which comes out
on Sargent Drive, a narrow winding road, passing a golf
course and through woods. Soon come to a narrow,
winding, hilly, rough road that runs north along Somes
Sound. Good vistas. Light traffic.

21.0 Left on State 198.

22.0 State 233 goes right to Bar Harbor.

22.7 Campground.

23.5 Left on State 102. Campground.

25.5 Campground.

27.6 Echo Lake Beach.

28.0 Campground and then come into Southwest Harbor.

29.0 Campground.

30.6 Left on State 102A. A rough, narrow road with light
traffic.

33.0 Camping supplies and hot showers.

33.6 Seawall Campground. End of second day.

0.0 *Third day* calls for an early start. Keep ahead on State
102A.

2.0 Campground and cafe.
2.5 Store. Pass through Bass Harbor and take a left on State 102. Setting is more open here.
7.3 Seal Cove Post Office and then turn away from the sea and head north.
11.4 Pretty Marsh picnic area. Just beyond keep right at a triangle with signs leading to Ellsworth.
13.0 Pass Round Pond on hilly, winding road.
15.2 Somesville. Left on State 102 North. This is a familiar route for a short way.
16.0 Keep ahead on State 102/198. Heavy traffic.
18.2 Left on State 102/198. Store.
18.7 Campground.
20.2 Left on State 3. Return 36½ miles on State 3 to Bangor and airport: 57 miles, or stop another night at the campgrounds at junction of State 3/198.

MASSACHUSETTS

As one of our smaller states Massachusetts provides very little remote bike touring. Population density doesn't allow this. However, there are plenty of fine biking miles through state forests, rolling hill country, pastoral farmlands and scenic coastline. Accommodations are plentiful.

In western Massachusetts the biker will find challenging rides in the Berkshire Hills and Hoosac Range. The Connecticut River Valley has splendid south-north biking on back roads. And the southeastern part of the state offers opportunities for historic pilgrimages to the towns and sites of our colonial past.

However, it is Cape Cod and the islands of Martha's Vineyard and Nantucket that is more "Massachusetts" than any other, save Boston. This is New England Coast at its very best. Small towns, long stretches of sand dunes, foggy days or sunlit seas and blue sky all seem to enhance the scene and add more charm to a land that is already appealing and exciting.

For those who would like to visit Boston and see the city via bicycle write for the map-folder *Boston Green Belt Bikeway,* Department of Parks and Recreation, City Hall, Boston, Massachusetts 02101.

For more information about Massachusetts as a vacationland

contact Massachusetts Department of Commerce and Development, Division of Tourism, Box 1775, Boston, Massachusetts 02105.

TOUR 12

Cape Cod is a very special place for bikers. There is so much to see and enjoy here that you should allow several days on this vacation island. Rather than suggest places to stay and length of days, only the mileage log has been included, noting services, campgrounds and AYH hostels. Hotels, motels, stores and restaurants are all along the route.

Location   Eastern Massachusetts.

Season   Spring, summer and fall. Spring can be cold; and always be prepared for those rainy and foggy days with bitter cold winds.

Transportation   Bus to Sandwich. Airlines to Hyannis. Although the tour starts close to Sandwich it could easily start from Hyannis.

A snug harbor on Cape Cod.

Rating   This is a good place for biking where many of the roads are wide enough to accommodate bikers and cars; some biking shoulders. And the local people are used to bikers. The terrain is mostly flat. The traffic is always moderate to heavy on US 6 and State 28, but congestion slows the traffic to 30/40 mph. This is easy touring.

Reference   Write for map-brochure, Superintendent, Cape Cod National Seashore, South Wellfleet, Massachusetts 02663. Many short bike trails outlined here for those who want to thoroughly see the park.

Tour Outline   150 miles, loop tour: about 3-4 days. The first thing to do is buy a detailed map of Cape Cod. They are available at many of the stores and businesses along this route. This will allow you to take any of the many side trips that lead down to the shore and smaller communities. The tour described here includes some of these on the first leg up to Provincetown.

0.0   Cross the bridge over Cape Cod Canal on US 6 State 3. Take a sharp right to State 6A and head for Sandwich, passing the bridge.

1.2   State 130 goes right to Shawme-Crowell State Forest: camping, showers.

2.5   Services along here. Road is busy but traffic is slow. Many roads go toward the water. Mix of homes and commercial. In these first miles there are countless antique and craft shops to visit; beautiful things here.

10.0   State 149 goes right.

11.6   State 132 goes right.

12.8   Pass under railroad bridge.

22.8   State 134 goes right.

26.8   State 137 goes right. Campground: showers.

27.0   State 124 goes right to Sweetwater Forest Campground: showers.

30.4   Nickerson State Park: camping, showers.

31.7   Pass under US 6 to reach Orleans. AYH Hostel here on Bridge Road. Bicycle shop in Orleans.

32.7   Left to Rock Harbor and cross over US 6. This is a narrow country road through residential area. Take a right at restaurant and art gallery and come back toward US 6 to make a

34.5   Left on Bridge Road to Eastham. AYH Hostel here after you pass Dyer Prince Road.

35.0   Right on Bridge Road. Marshes here have duck blinds and mosquito control boxes.

36.0   Bear left on Herring Brook Road. Good vistas.

37.0   Cross Samoset Road. Road is bumpy and narrow.

39.0   Road becomes Massasoit Road or West Road.

40.5   Drive-In Theater.

41.0   Left on US 6; campground south of here: Maurice's Tent and Trailer Park; showers. US 6 is an easy road to bike, although very busy. Wide enough for you and cars. Series of shops, eating places, lodgings.

43.5   South Wellfleet. Right at signs to Lecount Hollow and head to the sea and a landing: toilets. Then go back a few hundred feet to Ocean View Drive. Take a right and follow the beach. Homes here atop the dunes. Wind-blown shrubs and trees are stunted. Wonderful vistas.

45.5   Public access area.

47.5 Left on Gull Pond Road just where the road pitches down.

48.0 Keep right at fork.

49.3 Right on US 6.

50.5 US 6 becomes 2-lanes with a wide biking shoulder.

52.6 Truro. A right on Pamet Road will take you to AYH Hostel.

55.5 State 6A goes left. Keep right. North Truro. Three campgrounds in this area on South Hollow Road, Highland Road, Head of the Meadow Road.

61.0 Campground just before traffic light and your turn to the Visitor Center.

62.0 Visitor Center at Cape Cod National Seashore: exhibits and rest rooms. From here head into Provincetown, one of the most unique towns in America. Pilgrims first landed here before sailing across the bay. Whalers and fishermen made it successful in a commercial way. Then came the artists and the tourists and others who are restoring, building and giving new life to a charming vacation town. Its narrow lanes are lined with old houses, shops, galleries and fine eating places. Several days could easily be spent here. Indeed that's what many people do.

   If lobster is one of the reasons you came to Provincetown be sure to visit the Provincetown Seafood Market on Shank Painter Road. Bicycle shop in town.

   Pick up the return tour mileage at

62.0 Visitor Center.

63.0 Left on US 6 and return south along this good biking road.

81.4 West Road or Massatoit. Road goes right. Keep ahead.

84.6 Visitor Center at Salt Pond.

85.0 Fort Hill entrance.

88.0 Left on State 28, a 2-lane road wide enough for good biking. Services along here.

90.8 State 39 goes right. Keep ahead with moderate traffic. Sometimes you are next to the seashore.

96.0 Right on State 28, rather than going to Chatham. Traffic is slow but heavy beyond Chatham as you pass through several small towns.

99.8 State 137 goes right.

104.0 State 124 goes right.

107.0 State 134 goes right.

108.6 Cross Bass River into South Yarmouth. Good wide road

in a busy commercial area, all the way to Hyannis: AYH Hostel and bicycle shop. Beyond here road traffic lessens. More residential area. Roads lead to the shore towns here. You can visit Hyannis Port, Craigville Beach and Osterville before rejoining State 28.

120.0 State 149 goes right. More wooded, few homes.

122.0 State 130 goes right. Scattered commercial pockets.

124.0 State 151 right.

127.4 Childs River.

129.6 Cross Coonamessett River and come into Falmouth. Look for signs leading left to Sippewissett. This will be State 28A. Bicycles are not allowed on State 28. This is a good narrow road with light traffic. Mostly residential; beautiful homes and gardens. Trees overhang the road in many places. At other spots the water is in view as you pass through the small towns of Pocasset and Monument Beach.

140.0 State 151 goes right.

141.0 Left with signs to Pocassett and Monument Beach.

147.0 Intersection at Bourne. Follow signs to Providence and Boston on Trowbridge Road, reach a traffic circle at bridge from Buzzards Bay. Take road to Sandwich and Route 3. Heavy traffic along Cape Cod Canal but road is wide enough.

150.7 US 6 goes right to Hyannis and you are on State 6A headed for Sandwich. This ends the tour.

TOUR 13

Old Sturbridge Village is the highlight of this loop tour out of Worcester. However, before you get there you will take in some fine touring in the Massachusetts countryside. For the most part the trip winds through a setting of woods and rural farmlands.

Location   Central Massachusetts.

Season   Spring, summer and fall. Summer crowds on US 20 and at Old Sturbridge Village.

Transportation   Airlines and buses to Worcester.

Rating   Mostly light traffic, other than near Worcester and on US 20 at Old Sturbridge Village. Roads are generally good except in short stretches. The terrain is hilly, the toughest on US 202 with its long uphill grades. A moderate tour.

Reference   Write for information about Old Sturbridge Village, Sturbridge, Massachusetts 01566.

Tour Outline   103 miles, loop tour: 2 days, 1 night. Worcester is a city with full services, including bicycle shop. The airport is on the west side of town on a hill overlooking the city. Good views.

0.0 Exit airport and go left to take a long run down to a left on State 122, a 4-lane road through a shady residential area. Traffic is heavy. Soon the road narrows to 2-lanes with a biking shoulder; watch for sand.

1.8 Fruit stand.

2.0 State 56 goes left. Area remains residential; beautiful gardens.

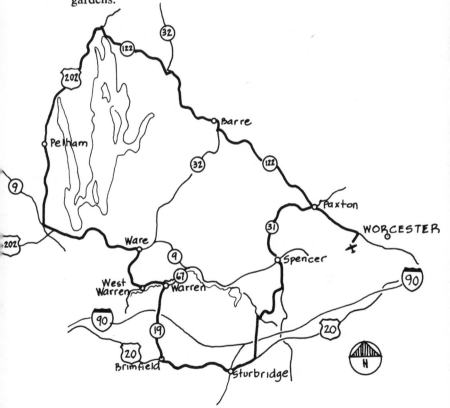

4.2 State 56 goes right and State 31 goes left. Town of Paxton: stores. Once beyond Paxton the route becomes more rural. Some dairy farms and homes in a country setting, wooded areas, short rise hills. Light traffic.

8.2 Intersection: sporting goods store and cafe. Then a long downhill run.

8.8 State 122A goes right. Pass over a lake.

9.6 Entrance to Rutland State Park: no camping.

11.5 Rest area.

14.0 Rest area.

14.3 Coldbrook Springs Restaurant.

14.6 Campgrounds.

14.8 Restaurant. More homes alongside road. Then pass through White Valley. Join State 32 from left and go on to Barre with its beautiful town square. State 62 goes right.

19.3 Fruit stand.

20.0 Rest area.

22.2 Spillway dam to right.

22.8 Rest area.

24.0 Left on State 122. This is a wooded route.

25.8 Pass lake. Road becomes more hilly: long downhill grades, short rises.

29.2 Pass rest area alongside parts of Quabbin Reservoir; a forested area.

31.6 Left on US 202, Daniel Shays Highway, a good paved road. Light traffic on a very hilly route through a mostly forested area. Scattered homes.

34.5 Restaurant and gas station.

37.2 Handcrafts of interest on right.

42.8 Vistas, just before entering Pelham.

43.0 Gas station and cafe.

49.0 Left on State 9. Stores and gas station. Eating places.

53.0 Entrance to Quabbin Reservoir and Dam.

54.2 Restaurant.

56.0 Rest areas. Road gets wider. Traffic is light; some trucks.

57.3 Vistas.

58.2 Restaurant. Residential area. Pass a cemetery and drop down to

59.8 Ware. State 32 comes in on right. In Ware look for signs leading to: The Warrens and Southbridge. Go right and leave town on a narrow, winding, hilly country road that is often covered overhead by trees. Vistas. Ware River on right below.

61.6 Fork: keep left and climb, then a long down hill to West Warren and a

64.8 Left on State 67 through town and alongside Quaboag River for a stretch.

65.3 Wayside area beside river. Then come to Warren.

66.0 Right on State 19 to leave Warren. Go under bridge and climb up out of town into the countryside on a winding, narrow road in a wooded setting.

68.4 Pass under I-90.

70.8 Pass town dump.

72.4 Left on US 20, a very busy road with heavy trucks.

74.8 Motel and campground: showers. End of first day.

0.0 *Second day* head for Sturbridge Village.

2.2 US 20 becomes a wide 2-lane road with more freedom for bikers. Traffic is slower.

3.1 Sturbridge Auto Museum.

3.5 Yankee Workshop.

3.8 Old Sturbridge Village. This is a reconstructed New England village of the early 1800's vintage. Viewers will see how the people of that time lived, worked and traded. Over 38 buildings of historical and educational interest to anyone wanting to know more about our heritage. Gift shop. Restaurant. Rest rooms. Open year round. Fee.
When you leave the Village go right on US 20.

4.5 State 131 goes right. Keep ahead on US 20 and pass under I-86. Pass entrance to Massachusetts Turnpike and keep right on US 20 East.

6.7 Left at sign to Wells State Park, cross over I-90 and pass entrance to Wells State Park. The road here is a broad 2-lane highway with wide shoulders for biking in open country. Enjoy it, because it only lasts a couple of miles.

10.0 Right at dead end, go a few hundred feet and make a sharp left to take a bumpy, narrow country lane in a wooded setting.

11.5 Triangle junction. Go left, then come to another triangle junction. Go right and up over a railroad bridge to a

13.2 Left on State 31, a wide paved road with moderate traffic; wooded setting.

16.0 Spencer: stores, keep on State 31, now an open country road.

20.5 State 31 becomes a bumpy country road.

21.5 Keep right on State 31.

22.0 Road widens and becomes residential.

24.5 Right on State 122. Then return 3½ miles to airport along same route of first day. 28 miles.

NEW HAMPSHIRE

Over 350 years ago Englishmen settled in Dover and Rye. Since that time others have been coming to this part of the country to enjoy living, working and playing along New Hampshire's rugged coast and in the mountains. The populated areas of the south offer the lure of beaches, pleasant biking in rolling hill country and the visits to small towns like Chesterfield and the Shaker village of Canterbury.

In the middle of the state there are numerous lakes with their summer resorts, good fishing and lake cruises. Visit Concord, New Hampshire's capitol and the center of the celebrated Concord Coaches (1813) that helped in our westward expansion.

White Mountain secenery is unforgettable, providing exciting touring on forest roads. Some steep grades here, but worth the effort. If your legs give out, take one of the trams or gondolas to those magnificent vistas.

Visiting bikers should write for the booklet *Bicycling in New Hampshire,* Box 856, Concord, New Hampshire 03301. It contains the outline of several trips in New Hampshire and Vermont including what to look for and suggested overnight lodgings. There is a descriptive list of AYH hostels along these routes.

TOUR 14

This is a tour from Nashua through southern New Hampshire countryside and along the seashore to one of America's earliest settlements, Strawbery Banke, in Portsmouth. On a sunny day the shore ride is lots of fun. Inland biking is very pleasant on the backroads.

Location   Southeast New Hampshire.

Season   Spring, summer and fall.

Transportation   Bus and airlines to Nashua and Portsmouth.

Rating   Traffic is generally light, or at least slow, in busy areas like the beach run north. The roads mostly have shoulders good for biking. Hilly sections are few and only of the short rise variety between North Salem and Seabrook. Consider this an easy tour.

Reference   Write for free information about Portsmouth and Strawbery Banke; Chamber of Commerce, 27 Vaughan Street, Portsmouth, New Hampshire 03801.

Tour Outline   60 miles, one way: 1 day.
A stop on the beach at one of the motels or campgrounds will allow for swimming and fun with a short bike the next day to Strawbery Banke.

Nashua is a large town with full services. A. U.S. Fish Hatchery here produces one-half million trout each year. In the 1840's Elias Howe developed his sewing machine here. The tour starts east of Nashua in Hudson at

0.0   Junction of US 3A and State 111 (Ferry and Library Streets) at a triangle park. Head east on State 111, a 2-lane road with room for biking. Traffic is moderate through a residential area.

0.7   Dairy Queen. Road is rough after here.

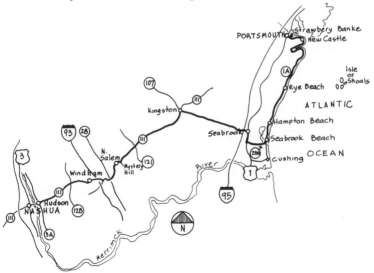

1.3 Left on State 111; road has a wide paved shoulder for biking. Sand here in spring. Industrial rural area that is soon left behind; traffic lessens.

4.0 Motel.

5.0 State 128 goes left. Store.

7.5 Road to Lowell, then come into Windham.

8.4 Motel.

9.0 Pass under I-93.

9.6 Left on State 111. Two stores here. Road is narrow, hilly and winding to pass Canobie Lake.

10.5 State 28 goes right. Keep ahead. Stores and Dairy Queen. Road is winding through lakes and residential area. Some sharp drop offs on pavement edges.

12.8 Delicatessen.

13.0 North Salem post office.

14.0 Make a sharp right and pass over bridge. Camping is to left.

14.4 Mystery Hill to right. This is a village of ancient stone structures. Research indicates their existence many years before settlers came here in 1640. Fee. Soon road widens with shoulder for biking. Rolling hills through woods. Vistas soon.

16.3 Cross State 121.

19.0 Cross State 121A.

19.2 State 111A goes left.

22.2 Road narrows as you come into Kingston, a town that is spread out. The Dr. Josiah Bartlett homestead is here. He was a signer of the Declaration of Independence.

23.0 Stop. Drive-In. Keep ahead through residential area.

23.5 Store.

24.4 Restaurant, then a

25.2 Right on State 107/125. Shoulder for biking.

26.0 Left on State 107, then State 107A goes right. Keep on State 107, a 2-lane, rough and winding road.

27.2 Interesting place of junk yard sculpture; worth a visit to see these humorous pieces.

28.0 Railroad and stores. Just beyond tracks State 108 comes in on right.

29.0 State 108 goes left. Drive-in eating. Road is winding and hilly now in wooded area. Good vistas of countryside. Light traffic on short rise hills.

32.3 Cross State 150.

34.0 Dog racing track. Go left and soon bike on wide shoulders.

35.0 Cross I-95 and go right on US 1 to pass through Seabrook: stores and services. Busy road with shoulders for biking. At a traffic circle take US 1 south.

37.2 Left on State 286, a narrow road that widens; shoulders for biking. Soon you are in sight of seashore. Cool breezes greet you here.

38.2 Camping on left as you cross marshes to the beach route ahead.

39.6 Left on US 1A. For the next few miles there are full services: food, lodgings, laundromat, etc. The road is easy to bike, but for those who want a quieter ride there are many streets that head for the water and parallel the beach in some areas.

41.2 Cross over bridge to Hampton Beach State Park. No camping. Beyond here there are all manner of recreational attractions, indoor and outdoor, as the route resembles a honky-tonk boardwalk. This is a real fun stretch for those who like a state fair atmosphere.

44.0 State 101C goes left. At many places the road is directly alongside the seashore, often with a seawall of steel or piled rocks on your right.

46.4 State 101D goes left. You are passing through an area of very fine homes, gardens and manicured yards.

48.5 Public beach.

50.0 Rye Harbor State Park: no camping. Eastward are the Isles of Shoals, discovered by Captain John Smith in 1614. Ferry leaves Portsmouth daily in summer.

52.2 Wallace Sands State Beach: no camping.

53.0 Small private pond with feeders for ducks. Black swan here, too. Beyond here the commercial scene is left behind as we go into marshy, wooded area and pass by Odiorne Point State Park: no camping.

54.4 Cross bridge on narrow winding road. Soon take a right on US 1B, a narrow road that brings you back to the sea again.

57.8 Cross bridge and pass Wentworth by the Sea, a resort.

58.0 Entrance to Coast Guard Station, and then come into New Castle. A turn to the right will take you to the waterfront. Homes here date back over 200 years. Look for the dates

Along the Kancamagus Highway.

on the houses. This was once seat of provincial govern-
ment.

59.5 Cross over bridge into Portsmouth.

59.7 Pick up first strawberry sign directing you to Strawbery
Banke. Go right and follow signs to restored Village.

60.2 Strawbery Banke. 60 miles. Strawbery Banke is the site
of the original town later to be called Portsmouth. In 1630
Englishmen came from London and Portsmouth, naming
the town Strawbery Banke because of the Piscataqua River
banks covered with strawberries. Now the town is being
restored, a 10 acre section of the old Portsmouth showing
visitors how our pioneer forefathers lived here in the
17th and 18th centuries. Shop of crafts and trades are
functioning. Fee. Full services in Portsmouth; bicycle
shop.

TOUR 15

The White Mountains are the background for this tour through
forests and mountain country. Vistas are magnificent. Roads like
the scenic Kamcamagus Highway are singular in our nation. Accommodations and services are everywhere, but their presence is
overshowed by the scenery of the countryside. Side trips can
include hiking, summer skiing, a gondola ride or an exciting

train ride to the top of Mt. Washington, the highest point in New England.

Location   Central New Hampshire.

Season   Spring, summer and fall. June can be cold but the tourists haven't arrived yet. Empty campgrounds and motels. September is wonderful.

Transportation   Airlines to Berlin Airport; daily from mid-June to mid-September. This airport is a few miles north of Berlin.

Rating   This is not all mountain biking, as it may seem from the area of tour. For the most part you are on flat to hilly roads, with good shoulders for biking. Climbing to Pinkham Notch, Kancamagus Pass and some of State 115 there will be some bike and hike, but the downhill runs make up for it. Nevertheless this is a tour for a practiced biker in good shape. Traffic is generally light other than near towns. This is a moderate to difficult tour.

Reference   Write for map-brochure of White Mountain National Forest, District Ranger, Saco Ranger Station, Conway, New Hampshire 03818.

Tour Outline   148 miles, loop tour.
About 3 days with overnight stays in motels or campgrounds as you tailor this trip to suit. Motels all along the way.

  0.0   Exit Berlin Airport and go south, then right to State 16, cross Androscoggin River and make a left on State 16. Village of Milan at this point. Stores. Road is narrow and downhill all the way to Gorham. Traffic is light. Setting is open with farms, scattered woods and houses along the way. The river has many small stone and wood islands, some with trees growing in them. These were used to separate the pulp logs on their way down to the mills in Berlin.

  2.5   Ahead is top of Berlin Ski Jump. Then pass by it.

  6.5   Full view of the industrial part of Berlin. Area is residential as you come to this very old town. Unfortunately it stinks as do all paper mill towns. The town is easy to bike through on a one-way route. White Mountains are in view now.

13.0   Gorham: stores, food and lodgings. Right on US 2, a

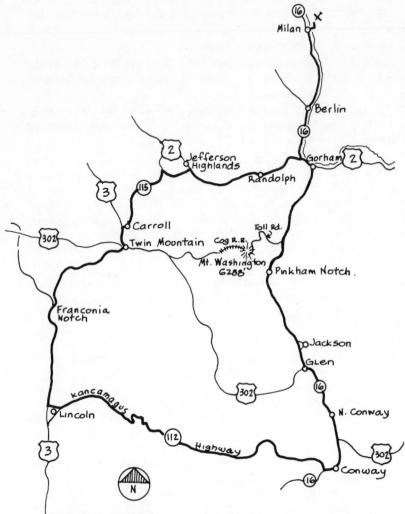

good road with a narrow shoulder. Services along this
road: food and lodgings.

14.1   Moose Brook State Park: camping.

14.2   Campground. Then start a very stiff climb. Good vistas
and then,

16.3   Down again with Presidential Range in view on left.
Crescent Range on right.

21.2 Road narrows to become rough, winding and downhill.

24.0 Rapunzel's tower—or at least it looks like it could be hers. Beyond here spectacular views of distant valley of the Connecticut River.

24.5 Campground. Left here on State 115, wide at first, then narrow as it winds its way over the valley floor beside the Israel River. Open farmlands and woods with the mountains surrounding. Very scenic.

27.0 Campground on Israel River.

27.5 Left on State 115 for Franconia Notch. Route becomes hilly and winding. Some stiff climbing here.

31.2 Good vistas.

31.7 Start downhill, passing through Carroll. Incorporated in 1832.

34.2 Campground.

34.7 Left on US 3: wide shoulders for biking. Heavy traffic. Many services along this road.

36.6 Pass US 302. Beautiful rock church with stone window frames.

37.0 Campground. Airport with air rides. Good vistas. Traffic is heavy.

40.5 Wayside area.

41.7 Cross Gale River. Then start long haul up to Franconia Notch. Wooded road. Scenic.

45.3 Mittersill Ski Area in distance.

45.5 Franconia Village to right. Then join I-93 and still climbing on long grades.

47.4 Food and lodgings, and then Franconia Notch State Park boundary.

47.7 State 18 goes right, then Echo Lake.

48.2 Cannon Mountain Aerial Tram. Rides here: fee. Very beautiful as you bike through the notch. New Hampshire Arts and Crafts Center. Then Old Man of the Mountain Center, a rock formation resembling a human profile. Then Profile Lake and then the long downhill from elevation 1896 feet.

50.4 Campground.

52.5 Cross Profile River and Appalachian Trail.

53.0 Pass Flume Picnic Area. Visitors Center. Restaurant, rest rooms and water. Covered bridges here.

55.3 Campground.

56.2 Campground.

56.8 Clark's Trading Post. Trained bears and old railroad. Turn left here for Kancamagus Highway. Pass through Lincoln on US 3A and then left on Kancamagus Highway. Traffic is heavy, but generally slow, 35-45 mph. This next 13 miles is bike and hike touring; the grades are tough.

58.6 Highway narrows as you go into woods and start climb alongside Pemigewasset River.

59.6 Loon Mountain Gondola Rides. Lodgings and food.

61.0 List of recreation areas on highway, then picnic area with water and toilets.

64.2 Campground.

70.0 Kancamagus Pass (2855) and then it's a long downhill run to Conway. Grades are steep at first and then level. Picnic area and overlook here.

70.5 On right: spring water out of a tube in mountainside.

73.0 Overlook. Beyond here grade levels off and its easy biking now.

76.0 Picnic grounds.

77.2 Campground.

78.6 Information Center.

78.8 Campground.

91.8 Swift River is on left.

94.0 Rough road here.

94.7 Campgrounds; Blackberry Crossing and Covered Bridge.

98.0 Leave White Mountain National Forest.

100.4 Saco Ranger Station. Left on State 16 to Conway with full services.

101.2 Left on State 16. Good for biking although busy with cars. Setting is very commercial. Some residential with woods. Views of mountains and Saco River in Washington Valley.

102.3 Campground.

102.7 Campground.

104.0 US 2 comes in on right as you come into North Conway. AYH Hostel here. Also bike shop.

104.3 Campground. Then an airport offering scenic air rides.

105.0 Red Caboose Cheese Shop.

105.5 Maple sugar house in operation. Good vistas to left.

106.2 Old railroad station at park.

107.0 Bicycle shop.

108.0 Scenic vistas: restrooms. Wonderful views up Washington Valley. From here on it's more of the same.

108.4 State 16A goes right.

110.0 State 16A right and road narrows down, not enough shoulder to ride. Starting to climb now.

111.5 Right on State 16. Wide shoulder for biking, but with patches of sand. Business establishments are fewer now.

113.7 Cross Ellis River and into

114.7 Jackson Village. Covered bridge. Jackson is "Ski Town USA". Nice shops and eating places open in summer. Road beyond is 2-lane with no shoulder; winding and rough in spots with heavy traffic. The setting is wooded.

119.7 Cross Ellis River. Steep climbing here beside the cascading stream. Some bike and hike.

122.7 Vista of Ellis River Valley.

123.7 Pinkham Notch (2032). The Appalachian Mountain Club maintains a camp here. Food and lodgings. This is a jump off for hiking in the White Mountains and along the Appalachian Trail. Also headquarters for spring skiing in Tuckerman Ravine.

125.6 Wildcat Gondola. Rides. It's all downhill now to Gorham on a wide road. Terrific biking if you can stand the speeds.

126.7 Mt. Washington Auto Road and Glen House Snack Bar. Rides up to Mt. Washington via station wagon. Fee. Beyond here road narrows.

128.5 Picnic grounds. Peabody River on left.

129.0 Campground.

132.7 Cross Peabody River.

133.0 Ranger Station as you enter Gorham: full services.

133.3 Left on US 2 and State 16. Androscoggin River on right.

134.7 US 2 goes left. Keep on State 16 for Berlin and airport: 13 miles.

NEW YORK

There is a lot of open countryside in New York, despite its large urban points. Vast roadless areas exist in the Adirondack Forest Preserve. It is here that hikers and canoeists find refuge from today's uptight life style. Bikers, too, can experience some of this by using the little traveled roads that lead to these more remote regions. Elsewhere in the state bikers will find enjoyable touring on the shores of Lake Ontario and the St. Lawrence River, or through the farmlands of western New York. Tourist information is available from State Department of Commerce, Travel Bureau, 99 Washington Avenue, Albany, New York 12210.

New York City bikers will want to read *The New York Bicycler,* by Rafael Macia. This is a slim volume of how-to and where-to information. List of bicycle shops in the New York area. 27 tours outlined with maps.

Utica has developed the first 5-mile section of a proposed Erie Canal Bike and Hikeway (Mohawk River). This is an operating canal running 348 miles from the Hudson River to Tonawanda just north of Buffalo. The bikeway has rest areas and comfort stations at two points.

TOUR 16

Here we have a nice weekend outing biking along the Delaware River and canoeing on the river, too. The route is from Port Jervis to Callicoon. There is a stop off at Fort Delaware. This scenic ride often takes you high above the river and then down to shoreline. A canoe trip for a day could make this be a fun weekend for those who like biking and boating.

Lake country in New York.

Location   Southern New York.

Season   Spring, summer and fall. Check about the spring water levels on the Delaware if you plan to canoe.

Transportation   Bus to Port Jervis.

Rating   Mostly light traffic on a good 2-lane highway that has many long climbs and downhill runs. A moderate tour.

Tour Outline   44 miles, one way: 2 days, 1 night.

0.0 Port Jervis has full services. Leave from Junction State 97 and US 209. Go north on State 97. The road is 2-lane and hilly with long grades up and down as it follows along the Delaware River. The shoulders are paved/gravel, good and bad. Traffic is moderate. Some heavy trucks.

1.9 Motel and restaurant.

2.5 State 42 goes right and traffic lessens on State 97. Sporting goods store. After here the road climbs to become a narrow shelf road with wonderful vistas of the river valley.

4.7 Store.

5.7 Stream and sign for Delaware and Hudson Canal which parallels the river: sections of it can still be seen along the

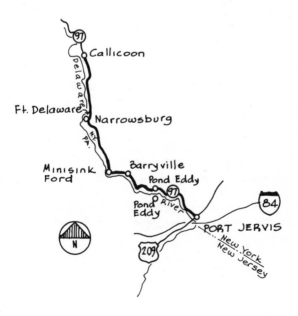

road. Once down alongside the river its beauty is apparent. Much of it is shallow and fast in a scenic setting as it courses south between forested ridges. Some summer homes on both sides of the river.

6.7 Motel.

10.0 Pond Eddy with the bridge over river to Pond Eddy in Pennsylvania. Climb again to nice vistas of the area.

12.5 Campground on river bank.

13.4 Parking area on left.

17.0 Barryville. Minisink Battlefield site is near here. State 55 goes over bridge here. Restaurant, stores, motels. Home-made chocolate just beyond here—worth a visit. And then once again you are along the river.

20.7 Minisink Ford. Toll bridge to Pennsylvania. Hotel and restaurant.

21.8 Waterfall on right. Stop for a few moments and enjoy the cool air.

22.0 Road leaves the river to start a stiff climb. Vista behind is wonderful, but that doesn't make up for the tough grade. Some bike and hike here.

25.8 Start long run down. Good vistas.

27.4 Camping, motel, restaurant.

30.0 State 52 goes right and then comes into Narrowsburg: full services.

31.6 Fort Delaware. This is a replica of an original stockaded settlement of 1754. It is a museum of pioneer life, a place conducted as an educational institution. Open weekends in June and September, daily in July and August. Gift shop, snackbar, restrooms. Fee.

39.0 Cafe.

42.3 Cross stream to traffic light. State 17B goes right.

43.7 Left at traffic light and down into the town of Callicoon: full services. Cross over railroad and go left through town to

44.0 Upper Delaware Campgrounds. 44 miles. The campground has complete facilities: store, laundromat, hot showers. They rent all camping gear. Of interest here is their canoe rentals: one or two day trips on Class I-II-III whitewater to suit your skills. They provide shuttle service and will keep your bike. For more information and reservations write Upper Delaware Campgrounds, Callicoon, New York 12723.

TOUR 17

Lake country. Vineyards and orchards. Large farms and rolling countryside above the lakes. Outstanding vistas and cool breezes. These are all part of this figure eight tour that runs through Ithaca over some of the best touring roads in America.

Location   Central New York.

Season   Spring, summer and fall. Fall colors are spectacular from these heights as you look over the lakes to the other shore.

Transportation   Airlines and buses to Ithaca.

Rating   Some very steep rises here as you leave lake shores. Once above lake route is mostly short rise hills. Traffic is light except on State 14 and US 20. Roads are very good for biking. Scenery is outstanding. Moderate tour.

Reference   For information about area write Finger Lakes Association, 309 Lake Street, Penn Yan, New York 14527.

Tour Outline   170 miles, loop tour: 3 days, 2 nights.
Ithaca is a college town (Cornell University and Ithaca College) at the base of a mountain on the southern shore of Cayuga Lake. Full services here. Bicycle shop. Buttermilk Falls State Park provides camping with showers, in town on State 13. Points of interest include the White Museum of Art and the DeWitt Historical Society Museum. The airport is on the east side of town.

- 0.0 Leave the Tompkins County Airport and take Warren Road south to a
- 1.0 Right on State 13, a 4-lane road with heavy traffic through a residential/commercial area: shopping center and motels. Soon drop down to Cayuga Lake and Ithaca. Great vistas of lake and the city on the hills.
- 3.5 Right on State 34, a narrow 2-lane road through residential area. Moderate traffic, lakeside homes, yacht basin. Very pleasant.
- 5.0 Start first rise, and its a tough one.
- 6.0 Top rise. Wonderful vistas of lake country. Setting is a mix of farmlands and residential.
- 7.8 Store.
- 8.4 Restaurant.
- 9.0 Left on State 34B at South Lansing. Stores.
- 10.6 Restaurant. Once away from the residential areas and into the open country the traffic is light. This is mostly a

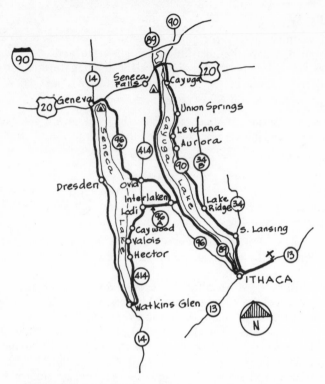

high road, from which you can see out over Cayuga Lake. Orchards, vineyards and dairy farming here. Very pleasant biking.

16.4 Lake Ridge. Cross a little bridge and pass County 156, to take a

16.5 Left at County 185, a rough narrow 2-lane road. Very little traffic. Pass big farms. Good vistas of patchwork farms across the lake.

18.5 Join State 90, a 2-lane road with wide shoulders for biking.

24.0 Long Point State Park: camping, swimming. Then start a long downhill run to lakeside and the village of Aurora. Many historical markers here, along with beautiful old homes. Inn and store.

29.5 Levanna, then a good biking road.

31.7 Store.

32.5 Union Springs. Stores, food and lodgings.

34.3 State 326 goes right.

38.3 Cayuga: restaurant and store. Alternate route drops down to the water and leads along it north to US 20; mosly dirt.

41.7 Left on US 20. Cross a bridge to pass Montezuma Wildlife Refuge and keep ahead to Seneca Falls and motels to end day. Campers go

43.5 Left on State 89, a 2-lane road with wide shoulders. Cross canal and come into residential area where shoulder is broken up.

46.8 Campground, store, laundromat, restaurant.

47.2 Cayuga Lake State Park: camping, showers, snackbar, swimming. Some inns beyond here.

0.0 *Second day* road in this section is lower and closer to the lake. The setting is more wooded. Homes and farmlands.

8.8 East Varick.

19.0 Pass County Road 141.

19.5 Right on County Road 141B to Interlaken on an uphill climb. Full services.

20.7 Left on State 96, then a right on State 96A, a 2-lane road with a rough shoulder in spots.

25.0 Lodi and go left on State 414. Stores, food and old hotel. Leave town on concrete road with good shoulders for biking. Vistas of Seneca Lake. Vineyards and cherry orchards.

29.2 Caywood.

31.0 Road narrows as you reach Valois. Cafe and store. Long climb out of town.

33.8 Hector: store.

34.2 Hector Memorial Park: camping. Beyond here there are several fruit stands.

38.5 Downhill to lakeside through wooded area.

39.0 Hector Falls. Motel.

41.0 State 79 goes left. Drop down to Watkins Glen: full services here. Bicycle shops. Watkins Glen State Park is on the south side of town: camping, showers, snackbar, swimming. Very scenic park with numerous waterfalls and grottos. This is also a car racing town; U.S. Grand Prix race in October.

42.4 Right on State 14 to leave town climbing on a good boulevard alongside lake. Motels and restaurants along here. Traffic is light, but heavy trucks service Watkins Glen from Geneva.

45.3 State 14A goes right and curves overhead. Divided highway ends here; 2-lane with good shoulders. Road is high again with wonderful vistas of lake.

47.3 Motel and restaurant.

49.5 Cross bridge. Campground.

50.8 Store.

53.2 Campground.

55.0 Restaurant.

55.7 Motel.

56.5 Morton Salt Mine.

56.8 Store, then a restaurant.

63.2 Cross bridge and enter Dresden: store and cafe. State 54 goes left.

65.0 Motel and store.

68.8 Campground, then store, motel and restaurant. Road becomes concrete with bad shoulder and area is more residential as you head for Geneva.

72.0 Store.

73.4 Cafe.

73.7 Come into Geneva: full services. Join US 20/State 14 through downtown, around waterfall to pass Seneca Lake Park: camping.

0.0 *Third day* stay on US 20/State 14 to a right on State 96A for Ithaca and Ovid, climbing above lake on 4-lane road and passing Rose Hill Restoration: a 19th century country home overlooking the lake.

1.8 Road narrows and you swing away from lake on 2-lane road with shoulders. Open countryside. Farms and some homes. Vistas.

2.6 Cafe.

5.6 State 336 goes left. Store.

8.7 Seneca Lake Campgrounds: showers.

10.8 Samson State Park: camping, showers, snackbar, swimming.

14.0 Motel.

15.5 Store and cafe, then come into Ovid: stores, cafe. Join State 96 here.

20.3 Store and cafe.

22.5 Come into Interlaken, go left on County Road 141B (Cayuga Street) covering familiar ground as you drop down to Cayuga Lake.

24.5 Right on State 89, a 2-lane road with shoulder for biking.

25.8 Campground.

26.2 Restaurant and campground.

30.3 Cross bridge.

30.8 Downhill through Taughannock Falls State Park: camping, showers, snackbar, swimming. From here on there are scattered motels, restaurants and stores to Ithaca. Very nice homes along the lakeshore. Wooded drive here.

34.0 Campground.

39.3 Bad road as you enter Ithaca. Pass a shoreline park to a

40.5 Left on State 79/89/96, then an immediate left on Buffalo street to pass the Station Restaurant and then a left on State 13. These roads are very busy with city traffic.

42.5 Pass junction of State 34 and continue uphill 3½ miles to airport. 46 miles for the day.

TOUR 18

Arching through the lake country of the Adirondack Forest Preserve this tour leads bikers into a northwoods setting from Glens Falls to Utica. Much of the route is forested. There are lakes to stop at for a swim or rest, and plenty of accommodations. The high ridges provide wonderful vistas from a cool vantage. The roads are a pleasure to bike.

Location   Central New York.

Season   Spring, summer and fall.

Transportation   Bus and airlines to Glens Falls and Utica.

Rating   The roads here are mostly excellent, some of the best in America for biking. Plenty of mileage with wide shoulders. Traffic is mostly light. The hills are generally not difficult except in some instances where the grades are very long. This is not mountain biking, but be prepared for a few tough climbs. A moderate tour.

Tour Outline   145 miles, one way: 3 days with overnight stops tailored to suit.

Glens Falls is a small town with full services: bicycle shop. The

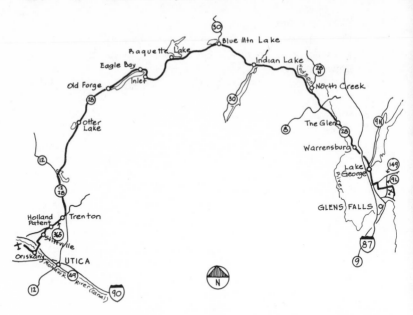

Hyde Art Collection is a free exhibit featuring the works of Rembrant, Renoir and many other great painters. In July and August an opera festival includes productions in English. The airport is on the east side of town.

0.0 Exit Glens Falls airport to go left and head north through the countryside. Farms and woods, scattered homes. Road is an easy 2-lane road, light traffic.

2.3 Left on County 35, drop down the hill and cross a brook into Warren County. Hills here with long grades.

3.6 Cross State 9L and keep left at fork in road to pass lake and reach a,

4.6 Cross over to Moonhill Road, top a hill and drop down to Nacy Road and a left on State 149. A hilly road here to a

7.4 Right on State 9. Eating place here. Start climbing on wide 2-lane road with biking shoulder. Heavy traffic. The road here to Lake George has many motels, restaurants, shops, stores, etc.

9.5 Vistas of Lake George below.

9.8 State 9N goes left, road widens and the setting is solid commercial and honky-tonk recreation. Lots of fun places:

restored Fort William Henry, Gaslight Village, Storytown USA and others.

10.5 Campground.

11.6 State 9N goes right. Keep ahead to pass under I-87 access to State 9N. Climbing now on easy grade; good road for biking.

13.3 Campground, then pass under I-87 into wooded route.

14.1 Road narrows to 2-lane but shoulders remain. Still climbing alongside I-87.

15.8 Enter Warrensburg: stores, food and lodgings. Campground across bridge.

16.6 State 418 goes left.

18.0 Leave town behind on a rough concrete road; shoulders not much good.

18.6 Campground.

19.7 Left on State 28, a 2-lane road with a broken shoulder for biking. Area is rural, scattered homes in open country and woods. Light traffic. Hills are short rise into long grades.

23.8 Hudson River on right as you come into The Glen.

24.5 Cross Hudson River and pass campground. Road beyond here is narrow and rough without shoulders. Secluded drive here in woods. Some long uphill grades.

28.5 Motor lodge. Good vistas.

29.0 Start long downhill run to cross Mill Creek.

30.0 Cross State 8 and continue on.

30.7 Cafe.

33.4 Restaurant and gas station as you come into North Creek on right, full services.

34.0 Good vistas as a downhill starts; wide shoulders. Pass a lake with a picnic area.

35.0 State 28N goes right. Open riding on good shoulders alongside Hudson River.

37.7 Cafe.

38.2 Store and cabins.

39.2 Store at North River.

39.8 Store.

40.5 Short rise above river; bike and hike.

42.0 Level off and start again; easier grade.

42.7 Level off and start again. Beautiful forest country.

44.0 Level off to rolling hillside. Great vistas.

49.0 Campgrounds and then long downhill to the town of Indian Lake.

50.5 Motel.

50.8 Cabins.

51.3 Indian Lake. State 30 goes left. Food, lodgings and stores here. Leave town on a good road with a bad shoulder. Some long grades.

53.0 Cross Cedar River. Then food and lodgings.

57.5 Road gets rough and remains hilly. Rooms and restaurant.

58.0 Hotel.

59.0 Campground on lake and then downhill run to Blue Mountain Lake. Food, lodgings, stores. This is a hiking center. Adirondack Museum; indoor and outdoor exhibits of local significance.

61.8 Left on State 28. Vistas of the lake. Leave the lake, climbing into hilly country through the forest. Grades are easier from now on.

68.0 Cottages.

70.5 Campground at Raquette Lake, a very beautiful lake. A lot of canoe camping is done in this area, from one lake to another. Canoe liveries.

74.0 Road to Raquette goes right.

78.5 Campground.

80.3 Seventh Lake.

81.7 Cabins.

82.0 Come into Inlet: food, lodgings, stores, laundromat and sea plane rides. Traffic is light.

83.4 Campground.

83.6 Hot showers.

86.0 Campground; then Eagle Bay, smaller than Inlet: food lodgings, stores.

87.0 Cottages.

91.5 Start steep climb to small pond.

93.0 Downhill run.

94.0 Campground, then come into Old Forge: food, lodgings, stores. Beyond here the road is good for biking as you leave behind the motels, shops, etc. associated with a resort area.

100.0 Marsh with beaver houses.

101.0 Campground.

104.8 Cross Moose River.

105.6 Food, lodgings, stores as you come into Otter Lake.

110.4 Pass White Lake. Road is now narrow and rough for a very short section. You leave the Adirondack Forest Preserve and the setting becomes rural with farmlands and open fields.

116.5 Motel and restaurant. Road is better.

117.0 Restaurant.

118.4 Cross Cayuta Lake.

119.7 Left on State 12/28, a 4-lane road with concrete median and bad shoulders. Heavy traffic. Scattered motels and eating places. Open countryside with marshes, fields of wildflowers and farms. Vistas.

125.7 Campground.

126.6 Restaurant.

127.5 Motel, then a diner.

129.0 Right on State 365 and drop down to Trenton: stores and eating places. Then stiff climb out of Trenton on a hilly ride.

133.5 Holland Patent: pleasant town square.

135.4 Left on State 291, and pass through Stittville.

137.4 Pass under RR bridge.

138.0 Right on Benton Road at signs directing you to Oriskany Battlefield. This is a narrow, rough, hilly road through open countryside. Very pleasant ride. Light traffic. Come to a stop sign and make a left and then an immediate right following signs to County Airport. Soon a left on State 49, crossing 4-lane State 49, the Erie Canal, railroad tracks and then right on State 69 (Erie Boulevard) following signs to County Airport.

142.8 Left at Oneida County Airport and it's a long climb to reach.

144.5 End of trip at airport.

PENNSYLVANIA

There's not much of this state that is inaccessible to a biker, and there is much of Pennsylvania that a biker will want to see. The eastern half of the state is mostly a series of parallel ridges, valley towns and farms in the Allegheny and Appalachian ranges.

The north-central area is the least populated. It is also a forested area with opportunities to bike into the "backcountry". Historied Pennsylvania is in the east, where much of the drama of the Revolutionary War and Civil Wars was played out.

Many counties publish maps outlining scenic auto tours. There are good basic routes here for designing bike tours that will include scenic sites and important historical points of interest. Of interest to bikers is information about Pennsylvania obtained from the Travel Development Bureau, Room 402, Department of Commerce, Harrisburg, Pennsylvania 17120.

TOUR 19

This tour takes you through the Laurel Highland Country of Pennsylvania, Johnstown to Mill Run. The 15 miles of State 381 below Ligonier must rate as one of the finest biking routes in America. The scenery is outstanding, the road comfortable enough and the traffic minimal. A great 1 day tour would be a return trip from Ligonier to Jones Mills and back. It is that kind of country—it should be done both ways!

And here we combine biking with canoeing and white water adventure. At the end of the tour stay overnight and try a raft trip on Stony Creek in the spring.

North of Mill Run is the spectacular Fallingwater, a residence designed by the late Frank Lloyd Wright. This is considered by many as the world's finest example of a private home. Tours; fee.

Location   Southwestern Pennsylvania

Season   Spring, summer and fall. Early summer for the color in the forest and wildflowers on the hills.

Transportation   Airlines and buses to Johnstown, east of Westmont.

Rating   The climb to Laurel Hill Summit is mountain biking, but after that it is a very pleasant tour, a downhill run mostly. The traffic is light and the roads generally good. This is an easy tour.

Tour Outline   45 miles, one way: 2 days, 1 night if you decide to go rafting.

Westmont is a town on the mountain west of Johnstown, the site of the 1889 flood that took 2000 lives. Westmont is a su-

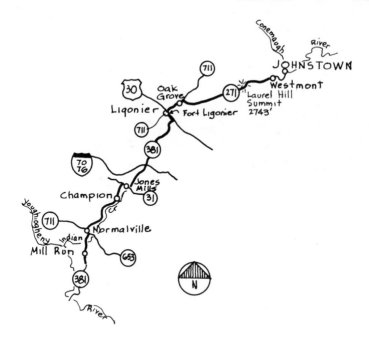

burbia of fine homes for people who can't stand to live in the hole below them. Tour starts at

- 0.0 Corner of Gardner Street and State 271; First Church of Christ Scientists. This is a very residential area. Beautiful homes and yards. Shady route with lots of room for biking on easy grade up.
- 1.3 Delicatessen and restaurant. Road narrows and starts down into woods, then a stiff uphill; bike and hike.
- 3.0 Top rise. Open countryside. Vistas and then another uphill climb.
- 3.7 Top rise.
- 4.0 Cafe, then downhill.
- 4.8 Right on State 271. Eating place. Route is still wooded. Vistas of hills and countryside. Still climbing to
- 7.5 Laurel Hill Summit at 2743 feet. Then start long downhill after one half mile. This is a very sharp drop on a good road that becomes rough after the main drop is ended. Great vistas!

13.0 Store as you level off, cross creek and enter a town. Beyond here it's all easy downhill to Ligonier.

14.3 Oak Grove. State 271 ends. Go left on State 711. Stores and eating places. Beyond here it is a mix of rural, homes and services all the way to Ligonier.

16.5 Enter Ligonier on city streets. Very nice downtown area with all the services.

17.2 Left on US 30. At this point is Fort Ligonier, a complete reconstructed fort used in the Indian Wars of the mid 1700's. George Washington was a young army commander stationed here. Museum and rest rooms. Fee.

19.0 Right on State 381. For the next few miles you travel through lands largely owned by Rolling Rock Farms and Game Preserve. Post and rail fences covered with roses border a shady, narrow lane that winds its way through hilly country. Beautiful grounds and estates. Open forest floor is covered with ferns and grass. A stream is nearly always close by. In October this area is the site of colorful steeplechase races.

21.5 Leave Rolling Rock Farms, but the scene doesn't change.

22.3 Cross bridge and make sharp left at signs: Southwest Field and Research Laboratory. Uphill is wrong way. Some open country here. Farms, vistas. Road has short rise hills.

23.0 Boy Scout Camp.

24.4 Left on Catawba Trail and into valley.

24.8 Southwest Field and Research Laboratory, then pass through a secluded forest ride in the Powderhill Nature Preserve.

25.5 Museum, and then a steady climb out with some bike and hike. Vistas.

27.5 Top rise and cross Pennsylvania Turnpike.

28.0 State 130 goes right, and start easy downhill.

31.7 Right on State 31/381 at Jones Mills. Busy highway.

32.3 Left on State 381/711. This is no longer the same road above Jones Mills. The countryside is the same but the highway is a 2-lane route used by trucks. Traffic is light on a mainly downhill run alongside Indian Creek. The setting includes more houses and services.

33.5 Seven Springs at Champion.

34.2 Campground and recreation center.

35.0 Log cabin of note.

35.4 Cafe.

36.0 Store.

39.8 Indian Creek Valley Picnic Area.

40.0 Cross Indian Creek and climb with a couple of stiff up and downs before reaching Normalville.

41.4 State 711 goes right. Stay left on State 381: store and cafe. Then drop into Youghiogheny River Valley. Vistas.

41.6 State 653 goes left. Cross Indian Creek again and climb into

44.3 Mill Run. Store.

45.0 House of Canoeing. Bike tour ends here where you can make reservations to canoe or raft on whitewater rivers: Class I to Class III depending on your skills. Go for a day or for a week. Everything included: equipment, food, guides. Shuttle service and a place to leave your bike. Overnight camping here, too. For more information contact Edward G. Coleman, 1286 Washington Street, Indiana, Pennsylvania 15701. Phone (412) 455-3703 in summer; (412) 465-2987 in winter.

TOUR 20

The destination of this tour is the Grand Canyon of Pennsylvania. Getting there from the Williamsport area is as good as being there. Exceptional scenery in narrow valleys and forested country. Secluded biking for the most part in an unpopulated part of the state. This can be a fishing trip for those Isaac Waltons who want to try their skills on the Pine Creek.

Location   North-central Pennsylvania.

Season   Spring, summer and fall.

Transportation   Bus and airlines to Montoursville.

Rating   Roads are generally not good. However, they are in areas rather remote and the traffic is very light. The hills are mostly short rise and there are easy gradients on all three days. This is a moderate tour.

Reference   Information about Pennsylvania's Grand Canyon can be had from Wellsboro Chamber of Commerce, Box 133, Wellsboro, Pennsylvania 16901.

Tour Outline   171 miles, return tour: 4 days, 3 nights.
Montoursville is east of Williamsport via US 220. Full services
here. The airport is in the city alongside the West Branch Sus-
quehanna River.

   0.0 Exit airport in a commercial/industrial area, cross RR
        tracks and reach US 220.
   0.7 Right on US 220 through busy downtown street.
   1.0 Left on State 87 through a pleasant tree covered street
        in a residential area.
   1.5 Right on State 87, following the Loyalsock Creek in farm
        countryside. Good paved road with a shoulder. Light
        traffic.
   4.0 State 864 goes right.
   6.0 Left on State 973, crossing Loyalsock Creek to start on a
        very hilly, winding route in a valley: farms, woods and

open countryside. A very scenic route with mostly short rise hills and a few big ones.

9.4 Top grade up from Warrensville. Short rise hills as you pass through Balls Mills to a

15.0 Right on US 15. Restaurant, cottages, motel. Heavy traffic with trucks.

17.2 Left on State 973, cross RR tracks and drop down beside Lycoming Creek. Just before bridge there is a large 1780 log cabin. More of the same scenic setting on a narrow, winding, hilly road.

18.0 Store.

22.7 Road widens and is smoother. Hills are not as steep.

26.0 Cross State 287. State 973 is rough now, along with hills and bends. Stiff climb out of valley to a drop down through woods to

31.6 Pass Tombs Run Church and level out to a right on State 44. Store at trailer park. You are now biking up the narrow Pine Creek Valley on a good road. Some short rise hills. Riverside homes along a scenic route that is mostly wooded. This is one of the best canoeing and trout streams in America.

32.2 Store.

32.7 Restaurant.

35.0 You rise above the river here on a shelf road.

38.6 At Waterville cross over Little Pine Creek and go right up along creek on rough road. Waterville has a hotel. End of day for motelers: 38½ miles.

40.0 Picnic area.

40.7 Happy Acres Campground: showers, store and cafe. End of day for campers: 41 miles.

0.0 *Second day* keep north to pass Little Pine Creek Dam. The floods in June 1972 passed 4 feet over the relief chute on the far side of the dam. The devastating torrents covered the roads and valley above. This rough road is an easy uphill grade in a very beautiful valley of open woods.

3.7 Pass School House Road.

4.7 Cross bridge.

7.8 Cross bridge and take a right to the village of English

Center; store. Take State 287 left, an easy biking road with light traffic.

9.4 State 284 goes right.

12.3 Top rise and then more ups and downs. Laurel blooming in open forest floor.

14.5 Motel, restaurant, store, then camping. Road is good enough up here for fast biking on downhill sections.

15.2 Cabins. Vistas here in open country.

16.7 Start long downhill to Morris.

19.0 State 414 goes left and come into Morris: hotel and cafe, stores, camp.

19.5 Left on State 287.

19.8 Campground. Then a valley floor road; easy biking with short rise hills. Soon climb again.

23.0 Road widens with paved sections added to road.

24.7 Store.

28.5 Start downhill to Wellsboro, passing dammed up lake to enter town on a boulevard with gas lights. Wellsboro is a very attractive town. Square in center of town has a statue of Wynken, Blynken and Nod in their fairytale boat. In mid-June they conduct a Laurel Festival. Full services.

30.6 Left on State 660 West and climb out of town on a good road.

33.5 Top hill and keep left on State 660 into the open countryside of farms, woods and scattered homes. Hills and vistas.

35.7 Campground.

36.6 Campground.

38.8 Methodist Church.

40.0 Motel, store, restaurant and campground.

40.4 Enter Leonard Harrison State Park with overlook of the "Grand Canyon of Pennsylvania". Outstanding vistas here of the 1000 foot canyon and Pine Creek. No fee. Trails, food, camping. The day ends here at the park campground or at the private motel or campground just outside the park. 41½ miles for campers. 44½ miles for motelers.

0.0 *Third day* return to Wellsboro, then down to Morris. At this point take a

21.4 Right on State 414, a valley floor road headed downhill

for the next 5 miles in a very scenic setting. A rough
road: light traffic.

23.4 Mountain water out of the hillside.

26.4 Cross Baab Creek into Blackwell. Hotel and food here.
Pass under RR bridge and reach Pine Creek coming from
the Grand Canyon of Pennsylvania. Cross Pine Creek
and take a rough dirt road alongside the stream in its
narrow valley. Very scenic. Road is good for biking.

29.4 High shelf road above the river.

31.4 Cross Cedar Run bridge onto rough, paved road. Pass
Cedar Run across river: store, meals and lodgings.

35.4 Spring water at hillside, and then cross Slate Run bridge.

36.6 Store. Right into Slate Run village. Hotel.

37.8 Campground at Cammal. Restaurant.

45.2 Hotel and food at Jersey Mills.

50.0 Join State 44 from right. State 414 ends.

51.4 Waterville: store and hotel. Or go north again 2 miles
to Happy Acres Campground: 53½ miles.

0.0 *Fourth day* head south from Waterville and return on first
day's route to Williamsport.

5.5 Left on State 973 for 32½ miles to airport in Williamsport following route of first day: 38 miles. An alternate
route leads down to Jersey Shore and along US 220 to
Williamsport: 28 miles for the day. However, this is a
very busy route.

TOUR 21

Allegheny National Forest is the setting for this loop tour out of
Warren, with riverside biking for much of the route. Several
options here for the biker who wants to go deeper into the forest
on good dirt roads. Within the Allegheny National Forest there
are many miles of well maintained dirt roads leading to spots like
Heart's Content Scenic Area.

Location   Northwest Pennsylvania.

Season   Spring, summer and fall. Spring may be too wet for
biking dirt roads in the forest.

Transportation   Bus to Warren.

Rating   Generally good roads with short rise hills. Two long
downhill runs to Warren and along Allegheny River. However,
some stiff climbs, especially out of Tionesta. Traffic is light on all

Pennsylvania countryside.

highways, but US 6 and State 66 have big trucks on them. Scenery is exceptional in the forest. This is a moderate tour.

Reference   Write for map-brochure of Allegheny National Forest, District Ranger, U. S. Forest Service, Marienville, Pennsylvania 16239.

Tour Outline   115 miles, loop tour: 2 days, 1 night.
Warren is a large town with full services: bicycle shop. Tour begins in downtown Warren at

- 0.0 Junction of US 6 and State 62. Leave town on US 6 West alongside Allegheny River on a very rough road with heavy traffic through residential area that becomes industrial.
- 2.0 4-lane road with median barrier: biking shoulder.
- 4.3 Move into countryside.
- 5.6 Right on State 62 and cross over US 6. Buckaloons Campground on right before crossing Allegheny River. From here on it's mostly downhill with short rise hills to Tionesta alongside the river. Riverside homes. Very scenic ride with light traffic.

8.2 Motel and restaurant.

12.3 Tan Bark Trail goes left.

13.3 Store, eating place, cottages.

13.8 Store, campground, cottages; very nice spot on the river.

16.4 Store, cafe.

20.0 Rest area.

20.6 State 337 goes right and then left. Stores, food and lodging here at Tidhoute. More hills beyond here.

22.6 Drinking water out of hillside.

27.3 State 666 goes left as you pass through East Hickory.

28.2 State 127 goes right to West Hickory.

33.3 Come ino Tionesta; stores, food and lodgings. Campgrounds. This is a vacation town.

34.0 State 36/62 goes right. Keep left on State 36, climbing steeply to pass the Tionesta Dam. Bike and hike here. If you make it to the top you will see a cafe with an airplane on the roof—no fooling!

36.5 Level off to a hilly ride in open countryside on a rough road. Vistas. Trucks, but light traffic.

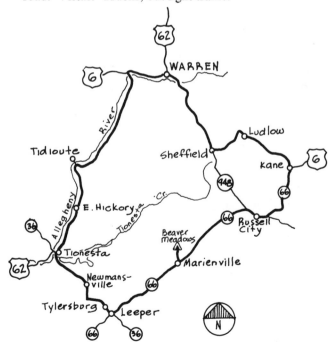

41.0 Store at wide bend to the right at Newmansville. Terrain is easier beyond here to Marienville.

42.8 Campground.

43.0 State 36 goes left. State 208 goes right. Store.

45.7 Tylersburg: hotel, store, eating place.

46.0 Leeper: store, cafe. Go left on State 66, a good paved road for biking. Once again road is more hilly and wooded. Light traffic, but heavy trucks here.

49.3 Restaurant and cabins.

50.0 Store.

53.3 Shoulder for biking and road is more level.

54.3 Store.

56.8 Cafe.

57.2 State 899 goes right.

57.7 Bucktail Motel; end of first day for motelers. Campers go into Marienville (stores, hotel, cafe) and take a

58.3 Left at the square 4 miles to Beaver Meadows Campground. Or go right 1½ miles to the Yearny Farm Campground.

0.0 *Second day* campers return to Marienville and head north on State 66, a good road for biking. Beautiful open country with woods, short rise hills and some stiff climbs.

1.6 Ranger station.

3.0 Fire tower.

4.5 Road is concrete.

5.3 State 666 goes left.

5.8 Motel.

6.8 Asphalt.

7.4 North Country Trail, then a stiff climb as you pass through a wonderful forest area where the trees arch over the road in sections. The open forest floor is covered with ferns and grass. Excellent chance of seeing deer as you bike along here.

10.0 Rest area: water.

12.2 State 948 goes left.

13.5 Store, eating place at Russel City. Beyond here the road gets rough and more hilly.

16.0 State 948 goes right.

16.8 Start long downhill.

17.8 Cross Twin Lake Trail, a bridge, and then start climbing for Kane.

19.6 Top rise and start down.

22.3 State 66 ends. Take US 6 straight ahead through Kane:
full services. Leave on concrete road and a route that is
mostly downhill to Warren, passing through mixed woods
and open country once away from Kane.

29.8 Ludlow: store, cafe. Out of Ludlow you can bike 7 miles
via Forest Service Road 133 to the Tionesta Scenic Area.
This is a 2,000 acre remnant of the original forest that
once covered 6 million acres on the Allegheny plateau of
New York and Pennsylvania. Some giant hemlocks are
over 400 years old; beeches at 300 years old.

33.8 Long downhill.

36.0 Sheffield; ranger station, campground, store.

36.2 State 666 goes left.

38.6 Across the RR tracks there is a bicycle repair shop in
someone's back yard.

40.0 Restaurant, store. From here on there is a scattering of
stores and services as you pass through Tiona, Weldbank,
Clarendon and Stoneham.

44.8 Campground, restaurant, motel.

46.3 State 59 goes right and you are again biking alongside the
Allegheny River. Cross the river and come into Warren on
a very busy road through town.

48.5 State 62 goes north and tour ends.

VERMONT

The flavor of Vermont is unique. The small towns, picturesque
farms, rushing streams and the background of green mountains
present an atmosphere of an unhurried life style. Indeed, the
roads seem to be less traveled, the towns not quite so busy, and
the people always ready to accommodate travelers with their
questions and needs.

The state has some outstanding scenery in its mountains and
northern lake country. It's eastern border is the Connecticut River
and most of its western border is shoreline also. As a historied
state it ranks amongst our foremost, having experienced the
colonial influence of the French from the north and the English
coming up from the south.

Bikers will want to get a copy of *Bicycle Touring in Vermont*,
Division of Recreation, Agency of Environmental Conservation,

Montpelier, Vermont 05602. This booklet contains general descriptions of about 20 tours, maps included. Tours from one to five days, 25 to 188 miles, with a state tour of 461 miles.

For related travel information write the Vermont Agency of Development and Community Affairs, Montpelier, Vermont 05602. Currently of interest would be the booklets, *Vermont Tour Guide* and *Vermont Visitor's Handbook*.

TOUR 22

Farmland and lakeside routes offer a good look at pastoral Vermont below Burlington. Easy biking most of the way in rolling hill country. The Shelburne Museum and the town of Middlebury provide interesting changes of pace if your pocketbook can stand the prices.

Location   Eastern Vermont.

Season   Spring, summer and fall.

Transportation   Bus, AMTRAK and airlines to Burlington.

Rating   Lightly traveled roads except for US 7. Good roads generally, with mostly short rise hills. Outstanding scenery along State 116 and the road next to Lake Champlain. This is an easy tour.

Tour Outline   90 miles, loop tour: 2 days, 1 night.

Burlington is Vermont's largest city, a lakeside summer resort center with views of the Green Mountains and Mt. Mansfield (4393). Full services here in a town that includes three colleges, fine museum of art and history, fashionable restaurants, antique shops and Vermont arts and crafts. Bicycle shop. The airport is on the east side of town.

0.0   Exit airport and go left on Airport Drive: residential area, store at entrance.

0.4   Cross US 2 on Kennedy Drive. Wide road with moderate traffic.

1.0   Left on State 116 and move south into countryside.

1.7   Cross I-89. Great vistas as you travel into rolling hill country: farmlands, woods, scattered homes. Adirondacks to the right in the distance. Road is 2-lane with light traffic and short rise hills.

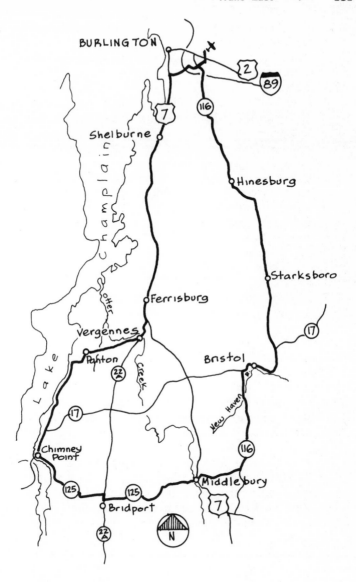

7.4 State 2A goes left.
10.0 Hinesburg. Cheese factory, store, then eating place on outskirts of town.

12.0   Start stiff climb.

13.7   Store.

14.0   Road gets rough and will be so in some sections. Good views behind.

17.8   Starksboro. Store.

23.0   State 17 goes left to the heart of the Green Mountains and the ski areas of Mad River Glen, Glen Ellen and Sugarbush Valley.

24.0   Giant stuffed moose head on a front porch. Surely the trophy head for Vermont!

25.0   Eating place. Road is smoother as you bike alongside New Haven River. Look for Prayer Rock. A former resident had the Lord's Prayer hewn into the rock to atone for the cussing of passing wagoners during the mud season.

25.6   Bristol: full services.

27.0   Left on State 116 south.

29.4   Cross New Haven River.

30.2   Store.

31.8   Campground, then enter into pleasant forest road alongside the mountains.

34.7   Right on Quarry Road for Middlebury: sign at intersection. This is a rough 2-lane, hilly road with light traffic. The area is a woods/farmland mix with homes of Middlebury citizens. After about 3 miles join Foote Street and come into Middlebury.

37.6   Left on Washington Street and reach the center of Middlebury: complete services here in this college town.

38.0   Junction US 7 and State 125. Take State 125 west, down and around the park to cross the river. Try lunch or supper in the very pleasant Soup Bowl on Bakery Lane. Excellent soup of the day, bread, ice tea with fresh mint sprigs and other delightful courses. Bicycle shop here. Visit the Sheldon Museum, a restored 19th century home. Closed Sundays; nominal fee. Visit Frog Hollow Craft Center.

38.3   State 23 goes right, then pass through campus of Middlebury College. Road out of here is narrow, winding, with short rise hills through a pastoral setting: farms, woods, some homes. Good vistas across fields. Light traffic.

46.0   State 22A goes left. Vistas of Adirondacks.

46.4   Left on State 125. Store.

50.4   Reach Lake Champlain and shore route.

52.2   Campground: showers, laundromat, store.

52.5   Store, cottages.

0.0   *Second day* continue north to pass

0.5   Chimney Point. Right on State 17.

1.2   Cabins. Some good examples of old stone homes in this area.

2.0   D.A.R. State Park: camping, showers.

2.7   Fork in road; store. Cottages to the left. State 17 goes right. Keep ahead on a narrow country shore road, through farms and orchards. Very scenic. Light traffic.

8.4   Turn away from lake.

9.7   Right to Vergennes. Ahead 3 miles is Button Bay State Park with camping. Rough road beyond here.

12.7   Campground and cottages.

13.7   Left on State 22A to cross Otter Creek into Vergennes: food, lodgings and store. This is one of the country's oldest towns.

14.0   US 7 is to the right. Keep ahead on State 22A to turn under a railroad bridge and reach a

15.4   Left on US 7, a wide paved road with good shoulders for biking. Heavy traffic and trucks. All the way to Burlington there are scattered eating places, motels, shops, etc. The setting is rural with farms, orchards and woods. Good vistas.

17.0   Road narrows; no shoulder (from here to Burlington there are occasional sections like this).

19.0   Cider press in operation since 1800. Covered bridge.

21.7   Mt. Philo State Park: camping.

23.7   Bicycle shop.

24.0   State F5 goes left, and then a long steady grade up. Good vistas.

28.5   Shelburne Museum: a unique collection of restored and duplicated American homes, covered bridges, lodges, barns, jails, sheds, mills, railway, sidewheeler, etc., depicting authentically the 18th century with its customs and style. Laid out on several acres as a town. It will take hours to see it all. Open May 15 to October 15. Expensive fee, unfortunately!

33.6   Right on I-189 East.

34.6 Left with Dorest Street and airport signs, then right with same signs to cross Dorset on Kennedy Drive and head for airport.

35.7 Cross State 116 and keep ahead 1 mile to airport.

TOUR 23

Mountain biking here with some hiking to get you over the big ones. The college towns of Bennington and Brattleboro are the base for this triangular tour. Scenery is exceptional in the mountains.

Location   Southeast Vermont.

Season   Spring, summer and fall.

Transportation   Bus to Brattleboro.

Rating   This is not an easy tour. Roads are generally hilly: 3 tough climbs. They are also mostly narrow with only a few stretches with good shoulders for biking. Traffic is mostly light except on US 7 and State 11/30.

Tour Outline   105 miles, loop tour: 2 days, 1 night.

Brattleboro is situated on the banks of the Connecticut River, in an area first settled in the early 18th century. Its once popular mineral springs were visited by Emerson and Harriet Beecher Stowe. It is no longer an agri-center, but has taken on the look of an industrial town. Full services here; bicycle shops. The tour begins in downtown area at

0.0 Junction of State 9/30. Leave town on State 9 west; bike and hike through residential area.

1.1 Cross I-91.

3.8 Leave Brattleboro on rough, narrow road; very hilly as it will be all the way to Bennington. Numerous eating places, motels and shops along this section. Pleasant route on an easy grade, some high rises, then some more bike and hike. Soon road

8.3 Levels off, then start another climb.

9.6 Marlboro College road. Motel and restaurant. Marlboro is home of the world famous Marlboro Music Festival, a summer event. The Marlboro Players Theatre is also located here.

12.0   Motel and restaurant with "100 mile view". Forest biking on a high rough road.

14.0   Hogback Mountain (about 2400). Food and lodgings and another "100 mile view". Then start downhill for Harriman Reservoir.

14.8   Motel.

15.4   Stark State Park: camping.

17.5   State 100 goes left. Store, then come into Wilmington, a pleasant town with shops, food and lodgings.

18.6   State 100 goes right, then pass Harriman Reservoir and start slow uphill alongside Deerfield River. Narrow road.

23.0   Cross Deerfield River.

24.0   Steep climb but not as bad as the climb from Brattleboro to Hogback Mountain.

24.7   Top rise, then start another climb.

25.2 State 8 goes left, then downhill to Bennington; good vistas.

27.6 Restaurant, store as you pass a couple of small lakes.

28.0 Woodford State Park Campground. Some short rise hills as you pass through Woodford.

31.0 Motel. Wide shoulders on road.

34.6 Road narrows.

36.8 Bennington: full services. Bicycle shop. Bennington was first settled in 1735. Be sure to visit Old Bennington with its 306 foot granite obelisk, 1805 church, the Bennington Museum and other interesting points.

38.3 Right on US 7 to leave Bennington on rough road with heavy traffic.

39.4 Road widens, services along here.

41.3 Pass under railroad tracks and move into countryside on rough road. Numerous services.

43.3 State 67 goes left.

43.8 Motel and restaurant. Fresh drinking water at roadside.

44.5 Motel and restaurant.

45.2 Motel and restaurant.

45.6 Pump at roadside.

46.0 Good vistas here.

47.0 Road to Shaftsbury. Road is more scenic now with fewer commercial establishments.

48.3 Campground.

50.2 Right on East Arlington Road. At this point end the first day. Either stay the night in one of the previous mentioned motels or campground, or continue (3 miles) into Arlington with full services and camping another 1 mile north of town on US 7.

0.0 *Second day* continue tour with a right on East Arlington Road; a narrow winding road through the countryside. Light traffic, very scenic.

0.5 Road leads right 4 miles to Topping Tavern Museum, a stagecoach stop in the 18th century.

1.0 Junction; keep straight ahead.

1.4 Junction. Keep right, cross two bridges and come into East Arlington. Keep ahead.

2.4 Covered bridge at Chiselville. There is a $1.00 fine for anyone who bikes over the bridge faster than a walk!

5.0 Road goes left.

5.8 Sunderland and store.

6.2 Cross Battenkill and railroad tracks. Along here there are some beautiful homes and large farms.

9.5 Right on US 7 and enter Manchester: full services.

11.0 Right on State 11/30.

12.0 Manchester Depot: bicycle shop.

12.7 Bicycle shop as you start climb: bike and hike section. Heavy traffic. Food and lodgings all along here.

13.8 Top hill, then start up again through forest.

15.8 Green Mountains National Forest, and climbing: more bike and hike.

17.2 Cross Long Trail/Appalachian Trail.

17.6 Right on State 30: more climbing on a good road. Light traffic all the way to Brattleboro. Good vistas.

20.0 Motor lodge.

21.2 Start downhill.

22.6 Restaurant.

24.2 Bondville. Food and lodgings. Entrance to Stratton Mountain, a very large ski resort.

25.9 Lodge.

26.0 State 100 goes left. Woody's Cracker Barrel Ski Shop: camping gear. Then short rise hills.

26.4 Motel and more small hills.

29.0 Start long downhill run to Jamacia; food and lodgings.

30.7 Jamacia State Park road leaves center of town: camping.

32.4 Cross West River.

33.7 State 100 goes right.

34.2 Country store.

35.0 West Townshend. Stores.

36.2 Vistas of hills and forest and river.

37.4 Townshend Dam.

37.8 Covered bridge.

38.2 Cottages.

39.2 State 35 goes left in Townshend and then a long downhill to Harmonyville; stores.

41.0 Cross West River.

41.5 Motel, restaurant.

43.0 Campground.

43.2 Cafe then store as you come into Newfane: stores, restaurant. Road is rough and narrow.

46.2 Downhill where Rock River joins West River. Good wide
shoulders here for biking along West River passing 1872
covered bridge. Light traffic. On a hot day a swim is in
order along here.

53.4 Pass under I-91 and come into Brattleboro. Heavy traffic.

55.0 Junction State 9/30 and beginning of trip.

CHAPTER 4

TRAILS MIDWEST

ROLLING HILLS, FARMLANDS, woods and flat open countryside characterize this region of states surrounding the Great Lakes. This land is criss-crossed with roads allowing for easy and moderate tours of lengths that will satisfy everyone. Predominantly a rural region, the towns and services are frequent. There are also many lakeside routes.

Bicycling's most popular event and trail are located in this area. In Ohio each summer there is the TOSRV, a 200-mile outing down and back up the Scioto River Valley, Columbus to Portsmouth on the Ohio River. Over 3,000 bikers participated in 1973.

The Wisconsin Bikeway stretches 300 miles through the scenic countryside of southern Wisconsin, LaCrosse on the Mississippi River to Kenosha on Lake Michigan, most of this is on rural roads.

Setting up camp.

ILLINOIS

The land of Lincoln is a prairie state offering good biking terrain and roads. Visits and tours here should include stops at the frontier village of New Salem, Cahokia and Cahokia Mounds State Park, Galena and the capitol city of Springfield.

Chicago has developed about 100 miles of signed bike paths, and safety routes through town for the commuter and recreationist. The lakefront route utilizes the existing walkways, passing through parks and by points of interest. For map-brochure write Chicago Park District, 425 East 14th Boulevard, Chicago, Illinois 60605.

For more information about Illinois write Tourism Division, Department of Economic Development, 222 South College Street, Springfield, Illinois 62706.

TOUR 24

Combining hill country and delta routes through sections of the Shawnee National Forest will give the biker a "good" feel for this most southern Illinois countryside. A visit to Ma Hale's in Grand Tower is a must; meals here are family style in a way seldom served today.

Location   Southern Illinois.

Season   Spring and fall. July and August will be too hot here.

Transportation   Airlines and buses to Murphysboro.

Rating   Half and half, as far as level and hilly roads are concerned. You'll have to be in shape. Traffic is mostly light except on State 149. Roads are generally in good condition. A moderate tour.

Reference   Write for map-brochure of Shawnee National Forest, District Ranger, Murphysboro, Illinois 62966.

Tour Outline   120 miles, loop tour: 2 days, 1 night.
Murphysboro is a small town with full services. The airport is east of town near the larger center of Carbondale: AYH Hostel and bicycle shop here.

0.0   Exit Southern Illinois Airport on airport road through farmlands.

1.7   Right on State 13 for Murphysboro, a concrete road with gravel shoulders. Open farmlands and woods.

4.4   Cross Big Muddy River and come into Murphysboro.

4.7   Left on State 127, a wide paved road. Light traffic.

5.0   Cross Big Muddy River and leave town through residential area,

6.7   Into countryside: short rise hills, wooded areas. Very pleasant biking.

10.3   Pass through Etherton, then some stiff hills. Vistas. Excellent road for fast downhill runs as you pass through Shawnee National Forest.

11.3   Cross bridge and start a long climb.

14.0   Road to Pomona Natural Bridge. Pass through orchards and farms. On the horizon ahead and to the right is the Bald Knob Cross.

17.7   Alto Pass and then road to the Bald Knob Cross.

23.0   Rest area: toilets.

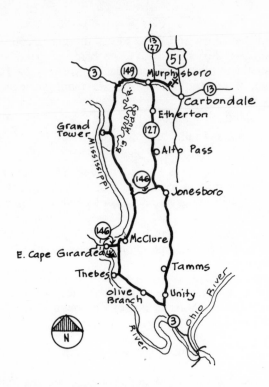

27.5 State 146 comes in from right: store. Then come into Jonesboro: cafe, stores, motel.

28.7 Back in the countryside on a good road. Setting is open and rural.

32.4 Road to Dongola goes left.

35.5 Cross Mill Creek.

38.0 Cross Hartline Creek.

43.0 Right to Tamms: store about one block in from highway.

44.5 Cross Sandy Creek and pass through Sandusky: store.

48.4 Store at Unity.

50.0 Right on State 3, a levee road in open country turning north. Very scenic as you pass through forests. Other levee roads go closer to the Mississippi River but they are usually dirt road. See *Reference* for maps that include these routes.

52.0 Wide paved shoulder for biking.

53.3 Cabins and eating place.

54.4 Motel. To your right are the yellow bluffs and Shawnee National Forest lands. Scattered homes in the area.

54.7 Olive Branch with stores and cafes.

57.2 Some short rise hills after this as you rise above delta country and enter into Shawnee National Forest again. Road is narrow, winding and rough. Scattered homes and farms.

61.3 Road to Thebes on left. Visit 1848 Court House in which Abraham Lincoln once represented a client. This courthouse, like all historic points in Illinois, is in disrepair because the state will not support restoration and maintenance. However, all these places are free of charge. Road gets better beyond here in forest setting: short rise hills.

63.7 Drop down from hills to delta and levee road through open countryside. This area was several feet under water during the 1973 spring floods.

66.5 State 146 comes in from left. Camping down the road about 3½ miles at East Cape Mobile Park: showers, laundromat, store. End of day: 70 miles.

0.0 *Second day* return 3½ miles to State 3 and head north to pass

0.8 Rest area.

2.0 Pass through McClure.

3.3 Motel, cafe, Some wooded areas after this. Bluffs and hills to the right.

11.6 State 146 goes right at Ware: store, cafes.

15.0 Wolf Lake: store. Camping just east of here in Shawnee National Forest.

15.8 Concrete road.

19.6 Cross Big Muddy River.

23.3 Campground as you come into Grand Tower: cafe and store.

24.0 Left is historic Grand Tower and Ma Hale's Boarding House where the cooking is family-style and worth a visit from any part of the nation. Entree, rolls, drink, desert and 9 bowls of vegetables—all for under $3.00! After eating—and you must make arrangements to do so, bike down to the levee and ride north a bit to the cliffs and old iron works. Store and laundromat in Grand Tower.

29.3 Cross over RR tracks.

31.0 Rest area: toilets and water.

32.7 Right on State 149, a wide paved road and grass shoulder alongside bluffs.

33.7 Cross Kincaide Creek and start a stiff climb on a narrow road to the bluff. Vistas. Road becomes hilly. The cuts through the hills have high banks on turned-up concrete curbs that make it difficult to leave the road if you have to. Don't waste any times on these sections. Scenic drive through woods and farms.

39.7 Lake Murphysboro State Park: camping. Then a more residential setting as you come into Murphysboro.

41.5 State 127 goes right. Return 4½ miles to airport: 49½ miles.

INDIANA

Indiana is a great vacation state for those who want to go it on their own. There are no spectaculars here. Rather it is up to

Covered bridge tours out of Rockland.

you to get out into the countryside on your bike and explore, discovering your own special places.

The Hoosier National Forests in the south provide a wonderful background for hill country bike tours. In the eastern part of the state it is the prairie country with its numerous lakes that is a popular area for biking. And throughout the state there are many fine streams for bikers who want a change of pace in a canoe.

Other points of interest include the Wyandotte Caves west of New Albany and Louisville, New Harmony with its history of communal living and education, Amishville near Berne, Mounds State Park near Anderson and the Michigan Lake shore.

Covered bridge buffs will want to visit Parke County, which has more covered bridges (37) than any other county in the country. Four color-signed tours lead out from Rockville ranging in length from 41 to 46 miles. This is all back-roads biking on some rough roads, but it is an excellent way to see the countryside. Very scenic. Caution: some of the signage is inadequate.

Also in Rockville there is a Museum of Covered Bridges on the town square. Booklets with maps and descriptions of the tours can be purchased here. If possible take your tour from the second to third weekend in October while a Grand Fall Festival goes on in Rockville.

The state produces a number of brochures outlining auto tours in different parts of the state. These are very handy in designing your own bike tour. Ask for *Indiana Side Tours,* Tourist Division, Indiana Department of Commerce, Room 117 State House, Indianapolis, Indiana 46204.

TOUR 25

This tour makes a nice day outing from Aurora south to Madison. The Ohio River is seldom out of sight as you travel down its valley through open farmlands and small riverside towns. A visit in Madison is a delight. If you plan to go there in early July be sure to be there for the big hydroplane boat races.

Location   Southeast Indiana along the Ohio River.

Season   Spring, summer and fall. Hot in the summer.

Transportation   Airlines to the nearby Cincinnati airport which is in Kentucky just across the Ohio River. Kentucky State 20 leads west to Aurora.

Rating   An easy tour on a downhill road that has a few short rise hills. The road is in good condition, but there will be some big trucks.

Reference   For information about Madison and its attractions write The Tourist Information Center, Vaughn Drive on the River Front, Madison, Indiana 47250.

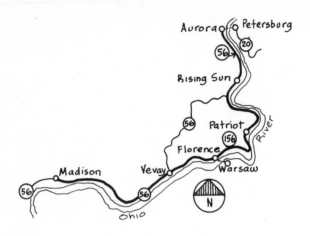

Tour Outline   56 miles, one way: 1 day.

0.0 Start tour in Aurora at junction of US 50 and State 56. Take State 56 out of Aurora through residential/indusrial areas to the riverside drive along the Ohio River. This is a downhill run with a few short rise hills. Much of this route is next to the water, passing through small towns, rich farmlands, riverside camps and homes. Some sections leave the river, but only for a short time. The road is mostly narrow, but lightly traveled. Some heavy trucks. A very scenic route.

3.3 Cross Loughevy Creek.

3.4 Camping.

5.8 Camping at riverside.

8.4 Rising Sun: full services in a small downtown area. Nice shady streets. State 262 goes right here.

11.2 Public boat ramp: toilets, then a campground and restaurant.

11.4 State 56 goes right, stay ahead on State 156.

20.5   Patriot: camping, store, cafe. State 250 goes right.

28.3   Ferry to Warsaw, Kentucky.

29.0   Florence: store.

32.7   Good road here.

36.5   Vevay: full services. State 156 ends. Take State 56, a wide shady route through town. Most of these towns have their own waterfront route to take as an alternate, soon coming back to the highway.

38.5   State 129 goes right.

41.0   Camping; store. Sections of road beyond here are occasionally hilly.

48.8   Camping, store, lodge.

55.0   Come into Madison.

55.7   Downtown Madison: full services. Go left at Mulberry Street to the waterfront and the tourist cener. Madison is another American town interested in preserving its past. In town are several excellent restored early 19th century homes reflecting architecture styles of the Federal, Classical Revival and Italian Villas. Walking tours, suitable for biking, will take you to the interesting homes and shops. Good eating and places to stay here.

Madison is also a sports-minded town with its own hydroplane boat, Miss Madison, winner of the 1971 Gold Cup. Big races held here in early July. America's only paddlewheel steamboat, the Delta Queen, passes here on its way from Pittsburgh to New Orleans. Bikers can plan to take their bikes with them on any trip aboard the Delta Queen. For more information about this unique vacation write Greene Line Steamers, Inc., 322 East 4th Street, Cincinnati, Ohio 45202.

There is camping at Clifty Falls State Park 1 mile west of Madison on State 56/7/107.

MICHIGAN

There is very little of this state that is not surrounded by water. Because of this and the many lakes and streams, the wonderful forested areas and the remote regions of the Upper Peninsula, Michigan bills itself as a vacationland. Add to these a system of good roads, moderate terrain and generally fine summer weather, and it becomes a bike tourer's vacationland.

In the Upper Peninsula tours might include stops at the very beautiful Tahquamenon Falls, The Pictured Rocks National Lakeshore, and towns like Copper Harbor. More roads are found in the Lower Peninsula, many of them lightly traveled and leading to places like Greenfield Village, and the Henry Ford Museum in Dearborn, Holland on Lake Michigan, and the many small lakeshore towns along Lake Huron.

For more information about visiting Michigan write Michigan Tourist Council, Lansing, Michigan 48926.

TOUR 26

Shoreline routes are often scenic, and this one is no exception. Visits to Mackinac Island and Fort Michilimackinac are highlights of this 3-day outing that heads north from Alpena to Mackinaw City.

Location　　Northeastern Lower Peninsula.

Checkpoint in Mackinaw City.

Season   Spring, summer and fall.

Transportation   Airlines and buses to Alpena. Buses to Mackinaw City.

Rating   Almost level roads with light traffic other than around Alpena. Roads are generally in good condition, except for the Presque Isle roads. This is easy biking.

Reference   At Fort Michilimackinac Visitors Center purchase a guidebook to Mackinac Island.

Tour Outline   100 miles, one way: 2 days, 1 night.
Alpena is a large town on Thunder Bay with full services. The airport is west of town on State 32.

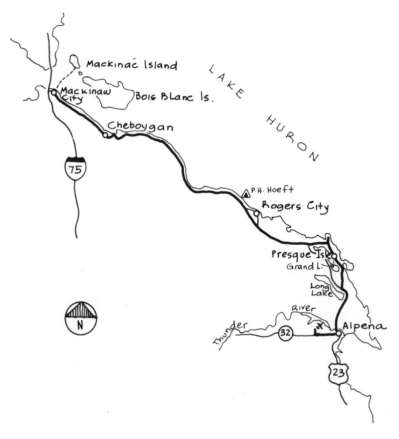

Exit Phelps Airport and take airport road to a

0.0 Left on State 32 headed for Alpena on a wide 2-lane road with a shoulder for biking.

2.6 Convenience store.

4.0 Motel. Enter Alpena along a nice landscaped parkway through a residential area.

5.5 Left at Truck 23 (Ripley Street) following the Thunder Bay River.

6.3 Left on US 23. Right here takes you to downtown Alpena: full services. This is a very busy road with room for biking.

6.7 Cross Thunder Bay River, then road is 4-lane for a stretch. Services all along here to Long Lake. Beyond here there are homes, farms and woods.

14.0 Store.

14.5 Store and cabins.

15.2 Right on signs: Presque Isle and East Grand Lake. Tavern on this corner. This road starts off good, then becomes a very narrow, winding, rough road in a very scenic setting. Little traffic here. Lots of birch in woods that hide homes and most of the lake front.

23.0 Better road.

24.0 Fire station.

24.5 Store and post office.

26.8 County 638 goes left and soon you are on a spit of sand sparsely covered with trees. Come to a laundromat, restaurant and store.

27.5 Lighthouse Museum of the original built here in 1840. Fee. Ahead is the new lighthouse, built in 1870.

28.5 Turn around and head back.

30.2 Right on County 638 which becomes a dirt road passing through woods.

32.0 Paved road and right on a remote route through woods.

34.2 Right on US 23, a 2-lane road; wide gravel shoulder. Light traffic as you head through woods, marshes and open country. Very scenic.

40.0 State 65 goes left.

44.4 Cafe.

45.0 Cafe and motel.

45.5 US 23 Business goes right 3 miles to Rogers City.

48.0 Cross State 68; a right here goes to downtown Rogers

City. Several motels and eating places after here. End of day for motelers. Beyond here Lake Huron is on your right all the way to Mackinaw City. At diffferent times the shore is in view. Settng is remote and scenic most of the way. Homes on lakeshore cannot be seen.

52.3 P.H. Hoeft State Park: camping, showers.

0.0 *Second day* continue on US 23 to pass a convenience store.

2.0 County park.

2.6 Motel.

9.2 Cross bridge; store.

10.2 Cabins and eating place.

10.4 Motel at fork in road.

10.8 Motel, then a cafe.

13.0 Motel; "last one for 20 miles".

16.0 Biking at water's edge along a very scenic section that includes a rest area: toilets and water.

22.2 Rest area: toilets and water.

23.2 Store.

28.0 Pass television station tower. The setting is more residential as you come into Cheboygan.

30.8 Cheboygan State Park: camping.

34.0 Cheboygan: full services for next few miles.

36.7 Leave commercial Cheyboygan behind and ride back into countryside alongside lake. Traffic is moderate and road is rougher. For the next while you will be able to see the distant tower structure of the Mackinac Bridge ahead at the end of US 23.

42.2 Rest area, then campground. From here to Mackinaw City there are scattered lodgings and restaurants.

46.7 Campground.

47.0 Store.

48.0 Campground. And then come into Mackinaw City. Two main attractions here: Fort Michilimackinac and the ferry ride to Mackinac Island. There are three ferries to choose from. They will take your bike. On the island check at the Visitors Center for the bike routes most suitable for you. The island is of considerable historic importance, featuring forts, buildings, etc. Several hours can be spent here on this very beautiful island, either walking or biking to historic sites and scenic points. Food and lodgings here

for tourers. At Fort Michilimackinac you can tour one of
the most authentic reconstruction in America: guided
tours, viewing of archaeology diggings, cannon firings. Fee.

TOUR 27

Few tours in Michigan can match this route for scenic splendor,
good biking roads and adequate accommodations. Biking north
from Manistee to Traverse City you will visit delightful towns
like Leland and Northport, the sand dunes at Glen Haven and
the Indian village at Peshawbestown.

Location   Northwestern Lower Peninsula.

Season   Spring, summer and fall.

Transportation   Airlines and buses to Manistee and Traverse
City.

Rating   Mostly good roads with light traffic. Some stiff hills,
but nothing to hold you back. This is a moderate tour.

Tour Outline   117 miles, one way: 2 days, 1 night.
Manistee is a small lakeshore town with full services. Fleet and
charter boat fishing here. Airport is east of town off US 31. Start
the tour in town at,

0.0   Junction US 31 and State 110. Head north on State 110,
a wide road with paved shoulder.

1.0   Sight Lake Michigan.

1.2   Orchard Beach State Park, then a store as road narrows
and becomes rough in spots.

2.0   Road is next to beach as you bike in wooded area amongst
homes. Very pleasant shady lane. Some hills and bends.

8.7   Left on State 22, a wide paved road with gravel shoulder.
Open country now.

10.3   Onekama: motel, stores, restaurants. Climb out of town
on a paved shoulder for a mile in the woods. Vistas as
you start down through orchard country. Good downhill
runs on paved shoulders. Cross marsh to Arcadia: store,
restaurant, motel.

21.8   Start steep climb. Top rise; vistas along here.

25.7   Store. This is also strawberry country; pick your own in
June and July.

29.8   Outskirts of Elberta.

30.2 State 168 goes left to ferry. Keep right to swing around bay and enter Frankfort.

31.4 State 115 goes right. Frankfort has full services.

32.0 City Park: toilets and water, then bike around Crystal Lake along a nice wooded drive with shore homes. A beautiful lake in the sunshine; access in spots.

36.4 Country store.

39.0 Leave Crystal Lake and pass Platte Lake.

41.5 Campground; store, cafe. Benzie State Park: camping. Beyond here there are a few hills to Empire.

53.0 State 72 goes right and pass through Empire: store, cafe. Empire is the western terminus of the Michigan Hiking-Riding Trail.

55.0 Left to Glen Haven on State 109, a narrow road. Vistas of Glen Lake and soon the big sand dunes. Most of the hills along this route are sand dunes piled here by ancient winds.
57.0 Motel and then D. H. Day State Park and dunes climbing.
57.3 State Park beach, concession, cafe, then motel.
57.8 Store and another motel. Some big farms in this area also.
59.6 Right on State 109.
60.0 D. H. Day State Park: camping, swimming. Motelers can pick one of the noted motels.

Second day continue east on State 109 to a
 1.5 Left on State 22 at Glen Arbor: store, restaurant, motels. State 22 above Glen Arbor is a narrow, rough road.
 5.0 Roadside drive-in eating.
 9.6 State 669 goes left to State Forest Camp. Store.
10.0 Restaurant, then homes alongside lake. Very scenic.
13.3 County 651 goes right, then come alongside Lake Michigan.
16.7 Pass market and bakery. Cottages.
17.0 State 204 goes right. Pass Lake Leelanau to Leland. This town is a must stop. Turn down at River Street and visit this unique waterfront. No more than a water lane, it has many craft and gift shops in rickety old fishing shacks: smoked fish, fresh fish, charter boats. The ferry to the Manitou Islands. It is a delightful spot to spend an hour or two. Public parking area and toilets.
      Country above Leland is more open and hilly. Vistas of farmlands.
25.3 County 637 goes right.
25.7 Restaurant.
29.8 Left into Northport and down to the waterfront. Shops, crafts, food and lodgings. A very pleasant town. Bicycle repair on the waterfront beside the unique Depot Restaurant. Public toilets and water here.
30.4 Leave waterfront and take State 22 south to Traverse City. Good road through open country, farms and homes and vistas of the lake. Light traffic.
35.7 Reach lakeshore again at Omena: store. Soon pass through Indian Village of Peshawbestown.
41.8 State 204 goes right, then come into Sutton Bay: full services. Concrete road beyond here.

48.3 Store. Beyond here more homes as you near Traverse City. More traffic.

54.4 Campground.

55.3 Come into Traverse City: all commercial setting now.

56.3 State 72 goes right. Keep on lakeside boulevard to downtown Traverse City.

56.8 Join US 31 and keep ahead. Park with rest rooms on left.

57.0 Reach Visitor Information Center. Zoo and city park across the road at lakeside. Traverse City has full services. Bicycle shop. Airlines and bus service here.

OHIO

In a relative sense few states have more roads than are to be found in Ohio. Besides a good network of superhighways there are countless miles of roads suitable for biking. And the state is interested in promoting bike touring. They now distribute a pamphlet describing several tours for day outings, 20-40 miles. Some counties are also providing guides to scenic tours in their

Ohio-Erie Canal at restored Roscoe Village.

area. For more information about biking in Ohio write Department of Natural Resources, Division of Parks and Recreation, 913 Ohio Department Building, Columbus, Ohio 43215. Ask for their brochure *Bicycle Journeys*.

TOUR 28

Hilltop vistas are your reward for making these grades—and some of them are tough! The rolling farm country is scenic in this area and best seen from roads like the ones on this loop tour north of Coshocton. A visit to Roscoe Village will be a highlight of the tour. If time permits stretch the tour to add an extra day of canoeing on the Mohican River.

Location   Central Ohio.

Season   Spring, summer and fall. Hardwoods make this a good fall trip for color.

Transportation   Bus to Coshocton.

Rating   This is hill biking over many short rise hills and some tough, long ones. The roads are generally good and traffic is light other than around Loudonville. Consider this a moderate tour.
Reference   Write for information about Roscoe Village Restoration, 381 Hill Street, Coshocton, Ohio 43812.

Tour Outline   93 miles, loop tour: 2 days, 1 night.
Coshocton is a small town with full services. Start tour on north side of town at junction of US 36 and State 83. Roscoe Village Restoration is one-half mile west on US 36.

   0.0 Head north on State 83, a good paved road leading into the countryside on a winding route. Some short rise hills, light traffic.

   0.3 Canal Boat Parking, part of the Roscoe Village Restoration. The canal boat Monticello takes a 45 minute round trip on the original Erie Canal. The Monticello is horse drawn. Across from here is a public recreation area with swimming, picnicking and camping.

   3.5 State 643 goes right. Most of this route is rising slowly while mixed with short rise hills.

   9.3 Steady uphill now for some distance to good vistas and a hilltop road.

12.3 Start downhill for Clark, then back up again to pass a lake so green that it looks fake from up high. The road beyond Clark is rough.

16.3 Store, then rest area; toilets and water, campground.

17.0 Cafe, then downhill to

19.0 Left on State 62 on rough, hilly road. Light traffic in open countryside.

20.2 Rest area; toilets and water.

20.8 Note roadside cottage made of junk and odds and ends.

21.3 Good road for biking.

23.3 Right on State 60, a narrow rough road that passes through Killbuck on shady streets. Stores and cafe.

24.3 State 60 goes left and cross Killbuck Creek.

30.3 Left on State 39/60. Store. Good paved road, but hilly with some long climbs. Vistas.

32.5 Home-made bread, pies, jellies, etc.

33.3 Start downhill for Nashville and enter on a rough road. Stores, cafe. Cross State 514 and leave town on a downhill run.

35.8 State 179 goes right and you are climbing again.

38.8 Start downhill to cross Mohican River, then some stiff up and down to

40.3 Top a rise and start down for Loudonville: full services. A vacation town for canoeists. This is end of day for motelers.

42.3 Left on State 3, following signs to Mohican State Park. Traffic is moderate.

43.3 Campgrounds, food and canoe rentals along here.

44.0 Mohican State Park: camping, showers, swimming.

0.0 *Second day* head west to cross the Clear Fork of the Mohican River. State 97 goes right. More canoe rentals here. Keep ahead on State 3 on a steady uphill grade.

2.7 Left on County Road 739, a narrow paved road. Very little traffic.

4.0 Fork. Go left on Knox County Road 43 and pass through open countryside. A delightful winding ride that is mostly downhill, with short rise hills for variation.

7.8 Left on State 514 to Greer, cross Mohican River and take a right down Knox County Road 77 alongside river. A shaded route on a very good gravel road. Stay in the cleared auto tracks.

10.0 Cross Mohican River again and leave it for awhile.

11.2 Mohican River alongside again.

13.0 Left to cross bridge into Brinkhaven: store. Pick up US 62 here and go left to cross RR bridge and pass old abandoned oil well.

14.7 Motel and food. Hills now rising to a

17.2 Right on State 206, and more climbing on a rough road. Vistas on this hilltop route through farmlands. Light traffic.

20.6 Tiverton Center.

24.3 Start downhill to Walhonding where you go left on State 206. State 715 goes right. Cross Walhonding River and make a sharp right, still on State 206. State 715 goes left. Start a long climb up to

27.5 Top rise, then

28.0 Right on US 36 through Newcastle and make a quick left on State 206. Store here. Fewer hills from here to a

31.5 Left on State 541 into New Guilford. Vistas with short rise hills and long grades on a rough road.

34.3 Cross State 79.

36.7 West Bedford: store.

37.2 Start downhill to

37.6 Meet State 60 at Tunnel Hill. Then State 60 goes left. Keep ahead on State 541. Road is very good now. Vistas are good but scenery is marred by strip mining.

47.5 Come into Coshocton through residential area.

48.0 Left on State 16/83 and continue straight ahead on White Woman Road to Roscoe Village a restored 19th century canal town on the Ohio-Erie Canal. No fees to visit shops and eat in this small town. Horse drawn trolley rides and boat rides. Excellent local pastries at the Craft and Bake Shop. At the end of the street take a right to State 83 then a left on State 83, a 4-lane road.

48.6 US 36 goes left.

49.0 Left on State 83. End of trip.

TOUR 29

The hills are easier in this part of Ohio, and this tour takes advantage of that. Hilltop vistas and farmlands are featured in this pleasant run south and back to Chillicothe. The Scioto River Valley is biked for about 22 miles above Portsmouth.

Location   South-central Ohio.

Season   Spring, summer and fall. Summer will be hot in this open country.

Transportation   Bus to Chillicothe.

Rating   Most of these roads are short rise hills or level. However, you have to get up to some of these roads and herein lies the rub; legs will get a good workout! The roads are half good, half bad. The traffic is mostly light except on US 52. An easy to moderate tour.

Tour Outline   120 miles, return trip: 2 days, 1 night.
Chillicothe is a large town with full services. The tour starts in town at the junction of US 50 and State 772.

0.0 Head south on State 772 through a residential/commercial/industrial area.

1.5 Cross Paint Creek and go right on State 772 alongside Paint Creek. Scattered homes, farms, woods and open countryside. Narrow, winding road.

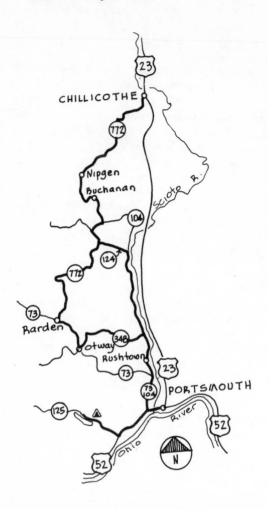

3.0 Store.

5.8 Store, then easy uphill in an open valley. Scattered homes as you pass through Brownsville.

9.5 Road begins to climb and becomes rough and narrow. Good vistas.

11.3 Store.

12.7 Road to Summit Hill.

13.0 Store.

15.0 Come into Nipgen: level road. After a drop and a rise it levels off again.

19.8 Downhill to Buchanan; store. Beyond here lots of ups and downs.

22.5 Level stretch on better road.

23.5 State 220 goes left. Keep right, rise some, then a major downhill to State 124 which goes right. Keep left on State 772, an easy valley road.

27.3 Left on State 124 a 4-lane road with a grass median. Route is smooth and downhill to

30.8 Right on State 104 on a moderately busy highway that parallels the Scioto River. This is the southern section of the well-known TOSRV: Tour Ohio Scioto River Valley. Every year thousands of bikers make the 105-mile tour from Columbus to Portsmouth and back on a 2-day outing. The road is a very good one, an easy downhill run to Portsmouth. The area is open farmlands with scattered riverside homes.

33.4 Cross Sunfish Creek.

39.5 Pass over Bear Creek.

40.5 Store.

42.2 State 348 goes right.

42.7 Restaurant, store.

43.2 Cross Scioto Brush Creek into Rushtown.

45.6 State 73 goes right.

48.4 4-lane highway. Food store and drug store.

49.3 State 239 leads right to US 52 and a 5-mile ride via State 125 to Portsmouth State Park for campers. Others cross the Scioto River where it joins the Ohio River and bike into Portsmouth.

51.0 Portsmouth: full services. Bicycle shop. Many motels and hotels to choose from in downtown area and along US 23. Note: there is also a fine motel on US 52 just before the State 125 turn off to Portsmouth State Park.

0.0 *Second day* leave Portsmouth or State Park and return up State 104 to a

9.0 Left on State 348, a narrow, winding rough road that soon becomes very hilly. Good vistas.

13.3 Road levels off awhile.

14.0 Store.

14.7 Climbing again.

19.2 Come into Otway. Right on State 73. Store and restaurant. Good road in a valley.

22.8 Rest area: toilets, water.

24.2 Come into Rarden: store and restaurant. Right on State 772, a very rough road, hilly and winding.

27.0 Top rise to bike easier grades through farmlands.

27.6 Store.

32.0 Store.

35.2 Store, then road becomes hilly again; starting long downhill.

39.0 Right, cross Sunfish Creek to parallel State 32/124 under construction.

40.8 Join State 124. Return 27 miles to Chillicothe via State 772, the same route you came down on. Or take State 124 to US 23 and return about 27 miles on an easier ride, but a much busier highway. 68 miles for the day.

Buckeye Trail follows distant ridge.

TOUR 30

Hilltop riding takes the biker into the state forest country of southern Ohio from Zanesville to Hocking Hills State Forest. No tour for those out of condition, unless you are prepared to bike and hike this peaceful tour along these ridges. Great vistas of the countryside.

Location   South-central Ohio.

Season   Spring, summer and fall. This is mostly open; hot in summer.

Transportation   Bus to Zanesville.

Rating   This is a strenuous tour, not because the hills are so high, but because there are so many of them. Good legs needed here on a very hilly route over fair roads mostly narrow. Traffic is light except around the Hocking Hills State Park on weekends.

Tour Outline   98 miles, one way: 2 days, 1 night.
Zanesville is a large town with full services. This is the site of the unique "Y" bridge. The tour begins at,

0.0   Junction of State 60/146. Take State 60 south through the town, passing along Muskingum River, a downhill run to McConnelsville in this narrow valley.

1.3   House on left with yard decorated and landscaped with found pieces and odds and ends.

2.0   4-lane road with shoulders. Traffic is moderate.

4.5   State 555 goes right.

4.9   Motel.

8.3   Duncan Falls. Stores and eating places, then road becomes 2-lane. The route is a mix of open country, woods, farms and riverside homes. The opposite river bank has many homes and camps on it.

12.8   State 376 goes left at Gaysport: store, eating place.

16.0   Better road in wooded section. Very scenic.

18.0   Drinking water on left.

18.4   Rokeby Lock: store and restaurant. A park beside the lock.

21.4   Store.

24.0   Beyond here the setting becomes more commercial as you come into McConnelsville, a leading salt producing center.

24.8   Right on State 78 into Malta. Cross Main Street and straight ahead. State 78 is a good paved road winding uphill easily.

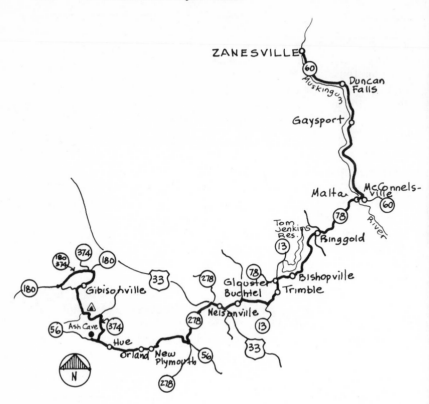

26.0 Left on State 78: still climbing out of industrial area.

26.6 Steep climbing.

26.8 State 377 goes left and you start into very hilly country—
one tough hill after another, passing farms, woods and
great vistas.

32.7 Start downhill to Ringgold where

33.8 State 555 goes right then left immediately.

34.6 Great vistas here on this ridge route. Part of the Buckeye
Trail follows this route.

37.6 Burr Oak State Park: cabins.

39.5 Burr Oak State Park: camping.

41.8 Store and campground at Bishopville. Beyond here it's
downhill to a

43.5 Left on State 13 and come into Glouster: store, restaurant, hotels. End of day for motelers. Campers stay at one of the campgrounds mentioned above.

0.0 *Second day* leave town on State 13. State 78 goes right. Park beyond here: picnicking, toilets, water. Then pass through Trimble. Traffic is heavy in this town.

2.0 State 329 goes left, then a rough road.

4.0 New concrete highway. Level ride in open country and soon make a right on old State 13 to a right on State 685, a narrow, bumpy road.

7.5 High rise hills in wooded area; bike and hike here. Then down to Buchtel and a

9.6 Left on State 78, a wide road. Light traffic on a level road.

10.0 Store.

11.0 Start up steep grade, then a sharp downhill to Nelsonville; store and restaurants.

12.0 Right on US 33, a busy route with room for biking.

13.3 Left on State 278, crossing Hocking River to pass through an old industrial area where there remain several beehive kilns at an abandoned brick factory.

14.0 Back in the countryside on a narrow, winding, rough road through woods. Light traffic.

16.0 Start climbing again.

16.6 Top rise.

17.0 Fire tower. Hilltop route now with good vistas. Farms and some homes.

21.0 Right on State 56, State 278 goes left immediately. Long downhill run on good road along a stream in a valley.

23.7 Store, then uphill on easy grades.

24.6 State 328 goes right. This section is easier as you drop into a valley through woods.

27.2 State 328 goes left at New Plymouth.

28.6 Orland: store. Hills again after this.

30.3 Start long downhill to

30.7 Cross State 93 and start another section with lots of ups and downs.

33.0 Long downhill to Hue. If you can get your speed up you can experience that elevator-drop sensation on some of these knolls in the road.

35.0 State 374 goes right.

35.3 Ash Cave of the Hocking Hills State Park: toilets, water and snacks. Return to a

35.6 Left on State 374, and start a very stiff climb, long and tough.

36.7 Campground at top of rise, then sharp downhill.

38.0 Start climb again.

39.0 Left on State 374/664.

39.6 Hocking Hills State Park: camping.

41.0 Eating place and store on hill top route.

41.4 State 664 goes ahead: keep right on State 374. More ups and downs and hilltop route. Vistas.

45.5 State 374 goes left. Keep ahead on State 678, an easier route that passes through Gibisonville, and then a long downhill to a

49.2 Left on State 180, a winding, hilly route.

49.7 State 374 goes right.

54.0 State 374 goes left. Keep ahead on State 180 to your parked cars and drinking water on right.

WISCONSIN

This is a biking state, one of the most active in terms of participants and facilities for bikers, including racing, touring and just good recreation. Summer weather, terrain, frequency of accommodations and an excellent system of secondary roads allow for countless easy and moderate tours through the countryside.

The Wisconsin Bikeway is probably the best known bike route in America. Certainly the section from Elroy to Sparta (32 miles) is one of the most popular. The trail here is atop an abandoned railbed, passing over trestles and through tunnels in a pastoral setting. Accommodations all along the way of this 300 mile ride across Wisconsin, LaCrosse to Kenosha on Lake Michigan. For more information write for the map-brochure *The Wisconsin Bikeway,* Department of Natural Resources, Box 450, Department B, Madison, Wisconsin 53701.

Milwaukee and *Oshkosh* are two Wisconsin cities that have designated bike routes in town. The local AYH laid out a 64-mile course in Milwaukee, hoping to see their bike route become the hub of a biking network in this region. The scenic route in

Oshkosh is about 16 miles, including lakeside biking and visits to the Paine Art Center and Arboretum, The Osborn House (1844) and statue of Chief Oshkosh.

Kenosha is the eastern terminus of the Wisconsin Bikeway. One of our country's bike racing tracks is here.

For more information about biking in Wisconsin contact Wisconsin Vacation and Travel Service, Box 450, Madison, Wisconsin 53701.

TOUR 31

Rolling country, dairy farms, orchards, and always the cool breezes from Green Bay on Lake Michigan. Summertime brings out the wildflowers along the roads and over the fields. Some very special and secluded sections to bike here in Wisconsin's Kewaunee and Door Counties. Fine vacation-resort countryside.

Location   North-eastern Wisconsin on peninsula.

Season   Spring, summer and fall. Cool biking in summer.

Wisconsin countryside.

Transportation   Airlines and buses to Green Bay.

Rating   Easy biking on mostly good roads with light traffic. Very few hills to give you any trouble. Easy tour.

Tour Outline   197 miles, loop tour: 3 days, 2 nights.

Green Bay is a large city with full services. The airport is on the southeast side of town.

0.0   Exit Austin Straubel Airport. Right on County GG, a rough, wide 2-lane road; lots of room for biking with moderate traffic.

1.3   County GH goes right.

2.0   Right on County GG at fork, into a residential/commercial area.

3.0   Cross Oneida Street.

3.5   Cross US 41 and go right on County H into an industrial area alongside the Fox River. Follow Fort Howard and North 6th Street to

6.0   Cross Main Avenue to one-way traffic that will lead you through downtown DePere and over the Fox River. Keep ahead on County G.

7.0   County G/X goes right through residential area.

7.3   Left on County G, and soon come into countryside on a good 2-lane road with wide gravel shoulders. Open countryside with farms and homes. Easy biking. Some vistas of Green Bay.

12.0   Left on County MM.

15.3   Left on US 141, then a right immediately on State 29, crossing the RR tracks into Bellevue. Store, cafe. Traffic is moderate on the good paved road, gravel shoulder. This is open dairy farmland. Big farms here.

17.7   County QQ goes left.

19.5   Poland.

20.0   Left on County T. Store and cafe. Light traffic here through open farmland. Some rough patching on the road.

21.0   Cross County JJ.

23.0   Cross County D.

24.0   Cross County N. Road becomes rougher in a more remote area.

25.8   New Franken. Store.

26.3   Cross State 54.

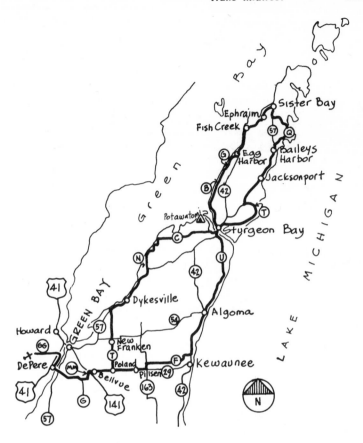

27.6 Cross County KK. Road becomes hilly as you near lakeshore.

30.5 Green Bay ahead, then downhill.

31.8 Right on State 57, a wide paved 2-lane; gravel shoulder. Moderate traffic.

34.0 County E goes right.

35.0 Dykesville: store, cafe.

35.2 County S goes right.

35.6 Motel, cottages.

36.4 County A goes right. Setting is open with a mix of lakeside homes and farms. Dirt roads lead down to lakefront at points.

37.8 Motel, restaurant.
38.7 County Y goes right.
41.0 County D goes right.
42.0 Cafe.
42.8 Left on County N; cafe. Keep straight ahead. Road is good for biking. Very light traffic. Open country, woods, a few big farms, hills with vistas of countryside and Green Bay.
45.3 County K goes right and you come to the water.
46.5 County park: water and toilets. Road is more winding.
47.3 Left on County N.
49.5 Left on County C, a rough road.
50.5 Right on County C.
53.0 County CC goes left; laundry and tavern.
54.0 Store.
55.3 Store: road gets narrow and rough.
56.2 Left goes miles to campground, setting becomes wooded.
57.5 County MM goes right in open country.
58.5 County M goes left.
60.0 Road leads about 3 miles to Potawatomi State Park: camping, swimming. This is the end of the first day for campers: 63 miles.
61.5 Leave County C and keep ahead into Sturgeon Bay, following along the waterfront. Left on Juniper and Larch to join State 42/57 in downtown Sturgeon Bay at the southside of the bridge. Food and lodgings here to the south on State 42/57. End of day for motelers: 62 miles. Sturgeon Bay is a boat building center. Dry docks handle lake steamers and ferries.

 0.0 *Second day* start at southside of bridge in Sturgeon Bay. Cross bridge and take County B out of town passing the boat building yards and a very nice residential area into the countryside. Some farms, woods, orchards, cafes and rental cottages along with lakeside homes. Very scenic area with light traffic.
 5.0 County OR goes right.
 6.8 Motel and then more homes.
14.4 County park: toilets and water. Keep ahead on County G now. Left on State 42 in Egg Harbor: full services in this resort town.

18.5 County E goes right.

19.6 Campground.

19.8 County EE goes right.

24.0 Fish Creek: stores, food and lodgings, another resort town.

24.4 Alternate route through Peninsula State Park will also bring you to Ephraim. Very scenic ride.

24.6 County E goes right.

26.8 County A goes right, then come into Ephraim on Eagle Harbor. Ephraim has an AYH Hostel.

27.2 Road from Peninsula State Park and alternate route, then Ephraim: stores, food and lodgings.

28.6 County Q goes right.

32.0 Right on State 57 before reaching Sister Bay, heading for east side of peninsula.

34.0 Left on County Q, to travel on a wonderful north woods route passing along North Bay and Moonlight Bay. Very scenic, with few signs of homes or farms.

40.5 Mud Lake Wildlife Area at Moonlight Bay.

43.0 Left on State 57 and come into Baileys Harbor: full services. County EE and F go right here.

45.0 County E goes right.

48.0 Wooded section of road.

50.4 Jacksonport: cafe, laundromat, store.

50.6 County A and V go right.

53.0 County I goes right.

55.0 County T goes right.

56.5 Left on County T: store and cafe, a rough road in open country.

58.6 Cafe where County T takes a sharp right. Now bike on the very beautiful Glidden Drive, a winding, narrow route through a wooded area of fine homes seldom seen from the road. Very scenic.

65.8 Gravel road.

67.2 Paved rough road.

68.4 Right on County T.

68.6 Left on State 42/57 and come into Sturgeon Bay.

70.0 Cross the bridge and end second day. Campers go on to Potawatomi State Park.

Third day leave south from Sturgeon Bay via a

0.0 Left on County U, also a section of the Hiawatha Pioneer Trail. Soon you are in the open country. Farms and scattered homes. Short rise hills.

3.5 Gravel road.

4.6 Paved road and easy rolling country. Vistas of Lake Michigan and farmlands.

6.5 County OO goes right.

8.7 Shore road now.

9.6 County J goes right as you bike along a bluff above the lake. Good vistas. Very light traffic; grass growing in the road cracks.

10.0 County park: toilets and water.

11.4 Shore road again, then a wooded section.

13.2 Left on County S. Good road through rolling hill country. Wonderful vistas as you approach Algoma: steeples in the town before you, with the lake on your left.

16.4 Algoma outskirts. Winery with tours here.

17.0 Left on State 42 to cross bridge and pass through Algoma. An alternate route is left after the bridge and down to follow the waterfront and soon rejoin State 42.

18.5 State 54 goes right. Then a city park.

19.6 County K goes right as you pass through a mix of residential and farmlands. Some lakeshore homes here, too. There is more traffic here than on most of the other roads you've been on. Some big trucks.

20.2 Rest area: toilets and water.

22.4 Motel and restaurant.

23.0 County D goes right at Alaska Lake: store and cabins.

24.7 County O goes right.

25.5 Restaurant.

26.3 Right on County F. Some stiff hills from here to State 163. Good vistas.

28.3 Cross County E.

30.0 Left on County C.

31.0 Right on County F. Store. County park: toilets and water.

34.0 Cross County B, rough road.

37.6 Left on State 163.

38.6 Right on State 29.

40.5 Pilsen: County V goes right.

41.4 County V goes left.

43.3 Cross County P: store.

45.2 County T goes right. From here you return 20 miles via first day route. 65 miles for the day.

TOUR 32

Touring through scenic farmlands on hilly roads is always a pleasant experience in Wisconsin. Touring south from Madison into Illinois bikers will pass through land settled by Norwegian immigrants, and the lead mining country near the Illinois border. The town of Galena in Illinois is an interesting one to visit. General Grant's home is here.

Location   Southwest Wisconsin.

Season   Spring, summer and fall.

Transportation   Airlines and bus to Madison. Airlines and buses to Dubuque, Iowa, 20 miles west of Galena.

Rating   Good roads. Many short rise hills atop ridge routes, with some big ones. Traffic is mostly light. A moderate tour.

Tour Outline   107 miles, one way: 2 days, 1 night.

Madison is a beautiful city built around two large lakes. This is Wisconsin's capitol. Full services here. The airport is on the north side of town.

0.0 Exit Madison Municipal Airport to take a right on State 113, a 6-lane boulevard that swings left to pass through a residential/commercial area. Stores, restaurants, homes. Heavy traffic.

2.5 Into open countryside with hills, farms, lakes and scattered homes. Vistas.

3.5 Left on County M, a 2-lane road; gravel shoulder. Setting is more rural. Moderate traffic.

5.0 Right on County K, a rough road with light traffic in open countryside; large, well-kept farms.

6.8 Cross County Q. Road gets better.

9.5 Cross US 12; store, cafe. Hills have long grades up and down.

12.3 Road becomes narrow and rough as you pass through a wooded section on a downhill run to a

13.5 Left on County P, a valley road that leads through Cross Plains.

16.3 Country store.

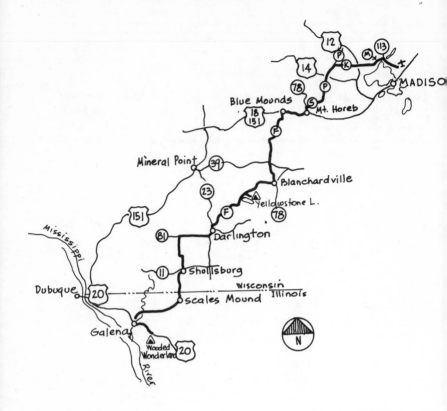

16.6 Cafe.

17.0 Cross US 14; stores, cafe, then start climbing in hill country to a ridge route: vistas.

20.5 Pine Bluff. County S comes in from left. Store.

21.4 Cross County J.

22.4 County P goes left. Stay ahead on County S.

25.5 Left on State 78 into Mt. Horeb; full services. Stop here for information about the area. A newspaper, *The Vacationer,* tells you about local attractions. *Song of Norway* production at Tryol Basin, nearby 1852 log church and other points of interest.

26.3 Right on US 18/151 and State 78.

27.8 State 78 goes left.

28.3 County E goes left.

30.0 County JG goes right.

30.3 County F comes in from right.

30.6 Rest area: toilets and water. Then left on County F before reaching Blue Mounds State Park. This is a short section of the Wisconsin Bikeway route.

32.3 Right on County F. County Z goes ahead to pass the Hauge Log Church (1852).

33.7 Rough, narrow road with short rise hills and vistas.

37.7 County H goes right; road is better now.

41.8 County A goes left.

42.0 Cross State 39.

46.5 Left on County F.

46.9 Right on State 78 into Blanchardville; heavy traffic.

47.0 County H goes right, then come into downtown Blanchardville: full services.

47.5 Right on County F. A stiff climb out of town. Vistas overlooking river and patterned countryside.

48.0 Top rise.

50.3 County K goes right.

52.0 County N goes straight ahead. Keep right on County F.

55.2 Left on road to Yellowstone Lake State Park. Campground is 1½ miles in. End of first day.

0.0 *Second day* continue on County F to a

1.3 Left on County F.

3.3 Right on County F/G/D.

4.5 County D goes right.

5.0 County G goes right, keep left on County F on some long grades; short rise hills here, too.

11.6 State 23 comes in on right and you ride into Darlington: full services. State 81 comes in here from left. Cross river where

12.0 County F goes right. Keep ahead on State 23/81. Good road through town.

12.7 Right on State 81. State 23 goes left.

17.0 Cross County U.

18.7 Left on County O, a good paved road over a series of hills as you head south into lead mining area and Illinois.

19.5 County Q goes right.

25.3 Cross State 11 into downtown Shullsburg.

25.5 Right on County O. City park with water and toilets; gold mine tours.

28.3 Cross County W.

30.3 Enter into Illinois on dirt road that passes west of Charles Mound (1235), highest point in Illinois. Dirt road ends as you enter Scales Mound. Keep straight ahead on Franklin Street to cross RR tracks, right and then left by the post office, tea room, store, cafe.

33.0 Right on Stagecoach Road for Galena, a ridge top route with great vistas, woods, homes and farms.

40.8 Sharp downhill to Galena River Valley.

41.6 Cross long bridge.

42.8 Galena, a historic hillside town with a levee and gates to keep out the flooding Galena River. Full services here; AYH hostel. Many old buildings to see here, including one of the oldest in Illinois (1826). General Grant lived and worked here in this mining country town. Cross the river and climb the hill to Grant's memorial home. A choice here of wonderful restaurants across from the home; a must for lunch or supper. Just beyond here on US 20/State 84 there is a

45.0 Motel: end of day for motelers. Campers continue on US 20, a wide paved road with moderate traffic; heavy trucks.

49.3 Camping at Wooded Wonderland, a unique farm that grows all crops organically. Store.

Third day head south along a ridgetop route with several rest areas and wonderful vistas of the farmlands below. Go out as far as it suits, then return to Galena. A return trip to Madison could include a visit to the restored Cornish miner's homes at Pendarvis in Mineral Point on US 151 in Wisconsin.

CHAPTER 5

TRAILS WEST

FROM THE ROCKY Mountains to the Pacific Ocean
bikers will find some of the most challenging, yet beautiful touring trails in America. States like California and Washington have
had many guide books written about possible touring routes.
Indeed, California must be considered *the* biking state in the
union in terms of numbers of touring bikers.

The Rocky Mountain states offer their own brand of spectacular biking on great plateaus and amongst towering peaks.
However, it's not all up and down here. The eastern parts of
Wyoming, Montana and Colorado are flat to hilly. Southern
Idaho, western Utah and Nevada are areas with easy grades.
Much of this area is a mile high and, while this is not prairie
biking, the hard climbs to peaks and passes are minimal. Arizona
and New Mexico are states where desert biking in the spring
can be a very colorful change of pace for the traveling tourer.

Starting the climb to K M Mtn. on Oregon coast.

ARIZONA

Arizona boasts more sunshine hours per year than any other state. Besides the spectacular Grand Canyon, bike tourers will want to consider visiting Canyon de Chelly, the Petrified Forest and Painted Desert, or the many ruins administered by the National Park Service. This state is dotted with historical towns and sites such as Tombstone, Old Tucson, Hopi Indian Villages and the Coronado Trail.

Much of the touring to be done in Arizona is at elevations above 5,000 feet. This makes for cooler biking in summer. However, drawbacks include poor roads and a scarcity of accommodations in a land where settlements are often many miles apart.

Phoenix is developing a 110-mile loop of hiking and riding trails that are open to bikers. Much of the system can be used now where it passes alongside canals once used by Indians 1400 years ago, through city parks and suburban areas. Look for petroglyphs on rocks. For more information write Maricopa

County Parks and Recreation Department, 4701 East Washington Street, Phoenix, Arizona 85034.

TOUR 33

Few places in this world compare with the natural wonders of the Grand Canyon. Couple this with a visit to Sunset Crater and the Wupatki Ruins and you have the ingredients for a very fine tour on the high plateau country north of Flagstaff. If time permits trips into the Canyon can be planned. Campers should have reservations, otherwise be prepared to camp deep in the woods away from the Ranger's scrutiny.

Location   Northern Arizona.

Season   Spring, summer and fall.

Transportation   Airlines and buses to Flagstaff.

Rating   The roads are not the best and some of the climbs are stiff. Winds can be a problem. However traffic is light, even in summer, except on US 180/State 64, Grand Canyon to Williams. This is a moderate to difficult tour.

Reference   Write for map-brochure Superintendent, Grand Canyon National Park, Grand Canyon, Arizona 86023.

Tour Outline   208 miles, loop tour: 4 days, 3 nights.
Flagstaff is a large college town with full services. Visitors can spend enjoyable hours at the Lowell Observatory, Museum of Northern Arizona and the Pioneers' Historical Museum. During the months of July and August a summer festival offers the very best in art, dance, films, music and crafts. International artists are featured. The airport is on the south side of town.

    0.0 Exit on Airport Road to cross I-17, then right on US 89A. Camping here at Coconino County Park. The area here is green and open with scattered forests. At about 7000 feet it is cool, although this is considered desert. Ahead are the snow patched San Francisco Mountains. Humphreys Peak is 12,670 feet.

    3.0 Pass under I-40, then under I-17 and take a right up and around to

    5.0 I-17/US 89/66 and go into Flagstaff (6905): full services for the next few miles. Busy traffic on this multi-lane road.

7.3 US 180 comes in from left, your return route. Then one
block on is the Chamber of Commerce: one more block
to a bicycle shop.

8.8 I-40 access goes right. Beyond here there are several
campgrounds.

10.3 Campground.

11.0 Left on US 89 for Page.

12.0 Shoulder for biking through outskirts of town.

12.6 Campground.

13.0 Campground, store and cafe. Then you are into the forest
and open countryside. Some big farms. Vistas of San
Francisco Mountains as you head north.

13.8 Two-lane road, rough. Traffic is light.

24.3 Campground. To the right are the cinder and lava dust mounds and hills.

20.3 Climbing here.

21.5 Top rise. Sunset Crater is on your right.

22.8 Right on road to Sunset Crater, a narrow, rough, winding road. Very light traffic. The dunes and hills are colored red and black.

23.6 Exhibit. Crater rim in sight. The forest floor is cinders and lava rocks with scattered pinyon pines, juniper and sage.

24.6 Campground and Visitor Center: rest rooms.

26.0 Lava flows overlook: Sunset Crater straight ahead. Some colorful vent cones.

26.5 Sunset Crater Parking: toilets. Trail up to crater rim.

27.0 Start long downhill through great dunes of ash and cinder. Scattered forest and open country.

30.3 Good wide road still downhill.

31.8 Overlook. Vistas of valley and painted desert. Toilets here.

32.3 On right there are other small vent cones.

36.0 Leaving Coconino National Forest. Open country as you pass over ancient lava flows. Vistas of mesa walls and valleys. The cinder cover is being replaced by earth and more ground cover. Wildflowers, sage and grasses.

39.3 Drop down sharply through redstone slabs into the

40.5 Wupatki National Monument.

42.5 Road to ruins (3 miles).

42.6 Visitor Center: ruins. Beyond here you bike down through a jumble of red rock, gullies and canyons as you pass over these green mesas.

43.6 Stiff climb up. Vistas behind of the ruins and Visitor Center.

44.8 Really stiff climb up to mesa. Great vistas here of countryside.

45.8 Top rise: ahead are San Francisco Mountains.

46.6 Viewpoint to left. On a sunny day the bottoms of clouds above the painted desert are cast pink. Easy biking here on top.

51.5 Citadel Ruins: in this area there are several ruins.

55.5 Right on US 89, leaving the Wupatki National Monument.

Wide road with light traffic: big trucks. Winds can be tough here on these long grades up and down. Cool.

66.0 Gray Mountain: motels, cafes, store. Soon you get vistas of buttes and mesas as you enter Navajo Indian Reservation.

69.4 Road narrows and winds through red rock outcroppings.

74.4 Store, cafe and camping.

75.0 State 64 goes left: Navajo crafts here. Keep ahead to Cameron and the Little Colorado River.

76.3 Cameron (4200): store, motel, cafe, camping and laundromat.

0.0 *Second day* head back to a

1.5 Right on State 64. Costumed Indian women and children have set up shop at roadside selling their beadwork. Sign here tells you that the national park campgrounds are usually full by noon. Road is narrow and rough, but lightly traveled. The area is open and hilly with the canyon of the Little Colorado on your right. On your left is the wall of the Coconino Rim. The color here is dark red with sage covering sparsely.

10.8 Little Colorado River Gorge Overlook.

14.5 Start the toughest climb of the tour. At this writing a new road is under construction. It is a much easier grade. As you climb you have magnificent views of the canyon country.

15.5 Indian Canyon Bridge; still climbing.

17.5 Little Colorado River bends away north to join the Colorado. Pinyon pine and juniper forest starting to show up.

19.5 Top rise, then some ups and downs to

23.0 Level biking across a plateau.

28.5 Enter Grand Canyon National Park: good road climbing stiffly.

31.5 Top rise: entrance station to park: fee. Campground, store and tower overlook. First glimpse of the amazing Canyon. It is hard to believe that over the ages this land has risen at a rate such that the river has been able to cut away this canyon without being trapped. Beyond here there are many places to view the Canyon at overlooks or by getting off the road.

34.2 Tusayan Ruins road.

38.7 Moran Point Road. Come into ponderosa pine forest now. Grass replaces sage. Yellow clover here; oaks, too.

40.5 Climbing stiffly.

42.2 Top rise to rolling hill route.

44.5 Viewpoint road.

49.0 Viewpoint, then stiff climb.

49.7 Top climb.

51.6 Yaki Point. Kaibab Trail head.

52.5 Right on road to Grand Canyon Village. Left returns to Flagstaff.

53.3 Elevation 7120 at Mather Point.

54.0 Yavapai Overlook.

54.5 Visitor Center: full services here, camping.

55.5 More services and then the road to the West Rim, a 7½ mile drive to Hermits Rest: refreshments and rest rooms here. Many vistas.

Third day can include a stopover with longer visits to Hermits Rest, a trip into the Canyon or a hike along the rim. Be sure to be at the rim at sunset.

0.0 *Fourth day* leave Visitor Center and head back to junction of State 64 to Cameron.

1.7 Keep ahead to Williams on US 180. Most people use this road to reach the park. State 64 goes left. All downhill now for 30 miles on a wide 2-lane road with lots of room for biking. More traffic on this road.

3.3 Entrance station.

6.0 Leave Grand Canyon National Park. Many services here; motels, store and cafes.

8.5 More services: motels, stores, cafes.

10.0 Campground.

10.5 Campground.

18.5 Down on open plateau, leaving forest behind. Ahead are San Francisco Mountains. Some uphill grades.

28.5 Left on US 180: motel, store, cafe, campground. This is a narrow road with light traffic across a plateau covered with scattered juniper, pinyon pine and sage. Some hills soon as you head for Flagstaff.

36.5 Cross cattle guard. Range cattle here.

44.5 Cross cattle guard.

55.7 Picnic grounds, then cross wide basin into a young ponderosa pine forest mixed with aspen.
69.0 Arizona Snow Bowl Road: motel here.
72.5 Leave national forest and come into outskirts of Flagstaff.
73.5 Museum of Northern Arizona: free.
74.5 Pioneers' Historical Museum: free. Residential area.
75.5 Right on North Humphreys with US 180.
76.2 Right on US 89 and back 7½ miles to airport. 84 miles.

CALIFORNIA

By virtue of population numbers and their disposition, California
must be considered *the* biking state. More guide books have been
written describing touring in this state than in any other. More
bikers are seen on the highways, and more towns have designated
bikeways, too. Cities like Palm Springs, Oakland, Newport Beach,
Santa Monica, San Luis Obispo have all tried to accommodate
bikers in some way.

The climate is generally favorable for biking, especially along
the coast range and in the eastern mountains. Winter biking is
possible throughout much of the state. Just stay out of the
central valley in the summer months. Be prepared for rain and
fog along the coast.

California Aqueduct Bikeway is a state water project benefit
for the states' citizens. At present writing there is a 70-mile
section open that parallels I-5 west of Modesto and Merced. Plans
are for a 400-mile route extending south. Facilities include those
for picnicking, sanitation and camping. A map-brochure is
available from the Department of Water Resources, Route 1, Box
39, Byron, California 94514.

Also at this writing the state is preparing a map showing
bikeways in California. Write Department of Transportation,
1120 N Street, Sacramento, California 95814.

Marin Bike Map is a unique publication outlining in detail
biking possibilities in Marin County. Maps and photos. Write
Group 7, Department B-9, P.O. Box 551, 7 Pixley Avenue,
Corte Madera, California 94925. $1.75 postpaid.

Yosemite National Park has a very active program for bikers.
The valley roads are most often used in outings that include
ranger interpretation tours and an annual bike rally. Bike

rentals are available and visitors are encouraged to park their cars and bike through the valley. Write Superintendent, P.O. Box 577, Yosemite National Park, California 95389.

Tour books of interest are listed here.

Bay Area Bikeways, by Standing, describes 21 bike tours in San Francisco and Marin County. Maps.

Bicycle Touring in Los Angeles, by Weltman and Dubin, describing 23 tours in and around the city. Excellent maps and photos.

Bike Riding in Los Angeles, by Marc.

Bicycle Trails of Southern California, by Kurk and Miller, describes tours in the area of San Diego, Pismo Beach and the desert.

California Bike Tours, by Gousha, describes in a general way 64 tours. Maps and photos.

Great Bike Tours in Northern California, by Ross.

J. J.'s Best Bike Trips, by Johnston, describing 20 loop tours around San Francisco and north of it. Maps.

50 North California Bike Trips, by Murphy. Maps.

Breakfast in Watsonville town square.

TOUR 34

Touring from San Francisco to Morro Bay includes some of the most scenic country in America. Big Sur, with its precipitous shoreline, Monterey and its wind-sculptured cypress, San Simeon, Morro Rock and a challenging shoreline road that clings to the plunging mountains, all help to make up the attraction this route has for so many bikers.

Location   California coast.

Season   Year-round. Be prepared for fog and rain. Summer days can be very cool.

Transportation   Buses and airlines to San Francisco and San Luis Obispo.

Rating   This is a tough one much of the way. Some very hilly terrain. Roads are not always the best and are often quite busy near urban areas. Other stretches of road are excellent with wide shoulders for bikers. This is a moderate to difficult tour.

Tour Outline   244 miles, one way: about 4-5 days.
Overnight stops are not recommended here, but left up to the individual.

Any visit to San Francisco should include biking through Golden Gate Park. A whole day can be spent here with stops to visit the gardens at the conservatory, the De Young Museum, the lovely Japanese Tea Gardens, the Academy of Sciences, or the windmills at the west end of the park. Sunday concerts are conducted at the music concourse. Canoe rentals are available on Stow Lake. This tour starts here at the west end of the park and the seashore.

0.0   Corner of Fulton and The Great Highway at the beach. To the north is Seal Rock. Head south along the ocean boardwalk. Access to beach here. On the left colorful homes are jammed together, many of them restored and remodeled to keep up appearances. Behind is the city rising up on the hills. You pass through Fort Funston. Lots of room for biking.

3.0   Right on Skyline Drive, passing Merced Lake, climbing up to look back on the city.

4.0   Road to Thorton Beach: not a through road as shown on some maps. Climbing now, passing residential area.

5.5   West Ridge Area.

6.0 Right at West Moor Avenue to take Skyline Drive south on a steep climb through a residential area.

7.0 Top rise, then a stiff downhill to the water.

8.5 Cross Monterey Road and keep on Palmetto Avenue, a frontage road next to freeway passing through Pacifica commercial area.

10.0 Left to go around park to follow freeway on Francisco Boulevard. Just beyond Fairway Drive at edge of park bike onto Bradford Way.

10.8 Join State 1, a 4-lane road with little room for biking. This is a very busy highway. Many services along here.

12.0 Rockaway Beach Avenue; services here next to bay. There are remnants of an old road clinging to the cliffs on the south edge of the bay.

12.5 Rest area: toilets and water. Then climb steeply away from beach up through woods and hills. Very scenic.

14.2 Top rise and come out to look over ocean. You are on the coast road. Great vistas. Many ups and downs here with light traffic and biking shoulder.

16.0 Views of Montara with its sandy beaches and colorful homes on the hills. This coast is softer than the one above San Francisco. The cliffs are lower and the exposed rocks much less. The low bluffs extend inland to make for great farming and grazing: sheep, cattle and dairy cows. Lots of services from here to Half Moon Bay.

17.0 Montara: restaurants, store, Coast Guard station and lighthouse. As is the case in other beach areas there are roads leading down closer to the water if you would like to take them.

18.2 Moss Beach: motels, stores, restaurants.

19.5 Airport. Road leads to Princetown, a scenic harbor town.

20.3 El Granada.

20.8 Half Moon Bay city limits. Below here the big farms show up and then a sign that says next services 25 miles away.

26.5 Leave signs of towns behind. You are in the countryside now with a biking shoulder and easy grades. Very scenic area as you bike near the ocean. Then some steep ups and downs as you alternately bike over headlands and down to the inlets.

32.0 Cross Tunitas Creek. Views up the creek. Valleys are very picturesque with farms patchworked against the hills.

35.5 State 84 goes left.

35.8 Cross San Gregario Creek: park with toilets.

37.0 Pass Pomponio Beach Park: toilets.

38.2 Pass pond on left.

38.6 Cross Pescadero Creek.

39.0 Road to Pescadero. Scattered homes along water. Farms on left. Easy biking. Lots of bird rocks offshore.

43.5 Art Studio and lighthouse in sight now.

46.5 Restaurant. Some sections of the road are 4-lane or 3-lane. In some areas the forest is close to the water. When you cross Santa Cruz County line you drop down to the water. High cliffs on left. Surfers along here, early morning to night, looking for the big one!

54.0 Public beach: toilets.

56.8 Cross Scott Creek.

57.7 Road goes left to Swanton, then railroad tracks alongside as you pass large cement plant at Davenport: cafe and store.

60.5 Road goes left to Felton. Railroad is between you and water now. Most of the homes are associated with the large farms.

67.5 Santa Cruz city limits: full services for the next several miles to Aptos.

69.0 Bay Street. A right leads to wharf area where there is an amusement park complete with roller coaster. Busy city traffic from here on.

69.8 Y-intersection. State 9 goes left. Keep right on Mission Street to pass Santa Cruz Mission and drop into downtown area and join Water Street to cross River Street and then the San Lorenzo River.

71.3 Join Soquel Drive and follow it to

72.3 Cross State 1 Freeway to 4-lane road with biking shoulder.

73.3 More residential area.

75.8 Cabrillo College: a wonderfully landscaped area.

77.3 Pass under RR bridge and come into Aptos Village: full services. Pleasant wooded drive to

78.0 Come along freeway.

78.3 Cross access to State 1 Freeway and continue ahead.

79.3 Right to cross State 1 Freeway at Freedom Boulevard and take a left on San Andreas Road through wooded section on a narrow road. Light traffic now as you pass farms, woods and

81.8 Stop: keep ahead through residential area.

82.4 Pass public beach: toilets. Then come out of woods into open countryside with very large farms.

83.3 Campground. Woods along here with open forest extending down to shore. Some vistas.

85.3 Sunset State Beach: camping on water. Then drop down onto the large fertile plains of the Salinas Valley.

87.3 Left on Beach Road. Light traffic.

88.8 Cross under State 1 Freeway and head into Watsonville through an industrial area.

90.0 Right on Main Street. Pleasant town square here. Full services.

90.8 Make bend onto Salinas Road as you pass through Pajaro and head around to a

93.6 Left on State 1, a 2-lane road with narrow biking shoulder. Heavy traffic as you bike by large farms.

96.3 Store.

97.8 Cross Elkhorn Slough, then come into Moss Landing: full services. Large power station here along with marinas and ship building.

98.6 Road to Moss Landing.

101.0 Castroville outskirts: full services here. Castroville claims to be the artichoke center of the world.

101.8 Right on State 1 Freeway to a 2-lane with biking shoulder. Heavy traffic.

104.5 Cross Salinas River. Monterey Bay.

106.8 Outskirts of Marina: full services here.

108.5 Freeway starts again so you must use Bike and Pedestrian path alongside freeway for next few miles.

112.8 Exit off Bike Path under State 1 Freeway to take Freemont Boulevard and head for Monterey. Continuing services.

113.0 Right on Del Monte Boulevard: 4-lane, busy traffic through commercial/industrial area.

114.3 Cross State 218.

114.6 Pass under State 1 Freeway.

115.8 Road to Carmel goes left. City park here.

116.3 Signs to Fishermen's Wharf. This whole area is a great tourist fun spot.

117.3 Right to Cannery Row and Pacific Grove and the coast road that will bring you to 17-mile Drive. After a couple of miles you will reach the beach and Ocean View Boulevard with its beautiful homes and landscaped shoreline. Pass Pacific Grove Park and wind along the shore. Some scattered homes.

121.8 Cove with sandy shore and surfers. Silica plant up on hill mars scenery as you leave the water to pass through a small community area.

122.3 Right to entrance to 17-mile Drive (straight ahead leads up and over Huckleberry Hill to Carmel and State 1). Fee is charged here for autos. Bikes are free. However, you cannot bike this one weekends or holidays. Moreover you can only go part way on the drive. Once on the drive you come right back to water and the south side of the cove you viewed minutes earlier. Scattered homes, a golf course and browzing deer; an idyllic scene next to the ocean. Seals in the ocean.

125.6 Seal Rock. Rest rooms.

126.0 Bikes prohibited beyond here. Left up Spyglass Hill Road, which becomes Stevenson Drive at the golf course club house, then becomes 17-mile Drive taking you by the Pebble Beach Golf Course and some large estates. Keep right to Carmel.

129.3 Exit at gate to 17-mile Drive on San Antonio Avenue to take a right at Eighth Avenue and down to Avenue of America forest shore road. This is a very narrow winding route through a shady neighborhood. Outstanding homes designs and landscaping. Wind sculptured pines and the homes blend.

130.8 Park: toilets. Then leave shore.

131.0 Right on 15th Avenue to pass the Carmel River School, the Carmel Mission built in 1770, and then a right on Rio Road to a

132.0 Right on State 1. You could have come straight here via State 1 (5 miles) from the turn off in Monterey. Road here is very busy: no biking shoulder.

132.3 Cross Carmel River.

133.4 Cross San Jose Creek: beach access with toilets. Views back to Pescardero Point and headlands.

134.3 Lobos State Reserve. Enter wooded area. Highway warning sign: hilly, winding and narrow road for the next 74 miles.

134.8 Pass through Carmel Highland and beautiful homes next to water. Side roads take you closer to the water. Some return, others are dead ends.

136.5 Cross Maliposa Creek. Country more open.

140.0 Cross Granite Canyon. At points along here the highway has been cut through the hills. Mud sides have been sculptured by the rains and winds to make some unique and interesting effects.

141.3 Cross Garrapata Creek. Wildflowers on the hillsides. The colors of the dark green trees, yellow grass, blue skies and ocean below make this all very pleasant. Coast road is higher than above Monterey. Mountains drop into the water more abruptly, not leaving much room for farming. Some sheep and cattle grazing.

144.0 Cross Rocky Creek: warning that you are traveling on a dangerous road. Then Bixby Creek. Climbing more here to higher elevations.

145.8 Round headland after a climb up from Bixby Creek and sight the big rock headland of Point Sur joined by a sand spit. Reminder of France's Brittany coast and Mont St. Michael.

147.8 Cross Little Sun River: cattle grazing here. Surfing also.

150.0 Entrance to Coast Guard and Naval Station. Cattle grazing on hills sloping gently to the water. Ahead are the Santa Lucia Mountains and Big Sur country. The road leaves the water and enters into the mountains and forests.

155.0 Motel, restaurants, stores, campgrounds: at this writing they had suffered a flash flood that wrecked many of the buildings. Food and lodging services for the next few miles.

155.5 Cabins, store, cafe, motel.

156.0 Motel, restaurant, camping.

156.8 Pfeiffer Big Sur State Park: lodge, food, camping, store. Beyond here you climb steeply. Vistas of Santa Lucia Mountains.

158.0 Cross Pfeiffer Canyon and still climbing.

158.8   Camping, restaurant, delicatessen. Top rise here and start down to pass Nepenthes Restaurant.

160.3   Cross canyon: restaurant and lodge. Road levels off and you bike along coast again over short-rise hills, then

167.3   Julia Pfeiffer Burns State Park and a number of creeks.

170.3   Pass Esalen Institute.

179.3   Enter Lucia: cabins, cafe. This is a small community on the mountain face.

181.3   Limekiln Creek: camping.

181.7   Los Padres National Forest.

182.0   Drinking water.

183.3   Campground: beyond here you are closer to the water.

186.3   Pacific Valley: cafe, store.

188.3   Campground.

191.6   Gordo: store, cafe.

194.5   Willa Creek.

196.0   Drinking water.

197.8   Drinking water.

200.0   Leave Los Padres National Forest.

201.3   San Luis Obispo County line.

202.8   Motel, cafe. Beyond here you drop down closer to water as you leave the mountains. Broad fields slope to the water. Grazing cattle and sheep.

207.8   Wide road: biking shoulder, the first since Monterey. It does not last long.

210.0   Motel, restaurant. Very scenic views of the distant lighthouse on the curving shore.

211.8   Piedras Blancas Light Station. Short-rise hills and easy biking on a narrow road alongside water. Lots of access to water. There are places here where the road has been moved back from the encroaching sea. The Hearst San Simeon estate is ahead on the left back up in the hills.

216.8   Come into San Simeon on a biking shoulder. For the next few miles there are many services, mostly food and lodgings. There is a road to Hearst San Simeon estate: public park here with toilets.

219.8   More of San Simeon: food and lodgings.

221.3   San Simeon Beach State Park: camping. Good wide road beyond here: biking shoulder. Motels.

223.8   Cambria: full services. Climb out of the hills beyond here on long grades.

233.3   Vistas include Morro Rock, your destination across Morro Bay.

237.0   Right on road to Cayucos: full services. Bike through town to join State 1.

240.8   Morro Bay city limits: full services, bike shop.

241.5   Atascadero State Park: camping.

243.0   Exit at State 41 to go under freeway and take a right on Main Street.

243.8   Pass under State 1 Freeway.

244.0   Right on Beach Street.

244.3   Waterfront and right to pass power station and reach Morro Rock.

TOUR 35

This mountain tour takes bikers into one of the most splendid forests in America. The giant sequoia trees are an unforgettable sight. The stiff climb from the Park Entrance (1700) to Grant Village (6200) in 16 miles is well worth the effort. Short mile-

Gleason Beach area and seal rocks.

age on the second day allows for visiting the special points of interest. Another day can easily be added, perhaps for a short hike. Note: the mileage shown for the first and second day is approximate.

Location   East-central California.

Season   Spring and fall. Summer in the valley is very hot.

Transportation   Bus and airlines to Visalia.

Rating   Traffic is light on these roads to and from the National Parks. Roads up and down from the mountains are narrow and very winding. This is a difficult tour.

Reference   Write for map-brochure, Superintendent, Sequoia and Kings Canyon National Parks, Three Rivers, California 93271.

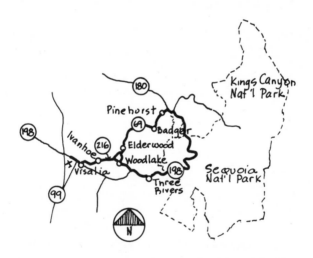

Tour Outline   143 miles, loop tour: 3 days, 2 nights.
Visalia is a town with full services. The airport is west of town.

0.0   Exit Visalia Municipal Airport to a right on State 198, a 4-lane road with room for biking. Heavy traffic. This is a basin area with industrial/commercial setting. Some farms.

3.0   Full services as you enter Visalia.

4.0   Bicycles prohibited on freeway. Go left and follow Main

Street into downtown through residential area and then into commercial area. Take a left on Court Street to take State 63 and then State 216 to Ivanhoe and Woodlake. This is easy biking.

11.0 Ivanhoe. Beyond here the yellow hills are on your left as you head through orchards for

19.0 Woodlake: full services. Cross State 245 and head

24.0 Left on State 198. Store here. Starting climb as you begin the long bike around beautiful Lake Kaweah. Steady grade and good biking road. Some recreation sites here with toilets and water. Very scenic. Leave the lake to follow a narrow road up alongside the Kaweah River, passing through Three Rivers (800) and by many motels and restaurants. This is a popular resort area. The peaks come into sight as you near the

39.0 Park Entrance (1700). Stiff climbing via switchbacks for the next 16 miles to the Grant Forest. Magnificent vistas as you pass two campgrounds and three watering stops. Traffic is light and slow on a narrow road. Many good views of the massive Morro Rock and surrounding peaks, many of them over 13,000 feet high. Soon you are passing through giant sequoias, a most memorable sight when first seen, and always a delight on return visits.

55.0 Grant Forest with its village, stores, restaurants and lodgings. In this area are some of the finest specimens of sequoias. Along the the Generals Highway is the General Sherman Tree, the largest living thing at about 3000 years old. This is the end of the day for those staying at a lodge. Campers should either stay at the earlier passed campground, Potwisha or Buckeye Flat, or go on the next four miles to Lodgepole.

Second day continue on for about 30 miles to Grant Grove. There are lots of ups and downs, but nothing like the first day as you stay at about 6500 most of the way. Pass two campgrounds and soon reach Grant Grove: full services. Also four campgrounds in area.

0.0 *Third day* head back by the Vistor Center to a

1.5 Right on State 180 to Fresno. Easy grade down on wide road. Traffic is light.

2.7 Big Stump Picnicking and Trail Head: toilets.

4.0 Elevation 6000.

5.2 Sequoia Lake.

5.7 Left on State 245, to Pinehurst (State 69 on some road maps), a winding downhill that leaves the park and continues down through the forest. The vistas aren't what they were on the other climb.

8.5 Unusual cafe stuck in the side of the mountain. Careful, or you will miss it! Vistas of mesas and hills below. Some scattered homes.

10.0 Pinehurst: El. 4100. Cafe, cabins, store.

11.7 At fork: left on State 245. Right goes up to Badger.

12.7 Grade eases off. Oaks and grass now.

14.7 Vistas of peaks behind and to the left as you climb some to reach

16.2 Badger: restaurant and motel. Then downhill again through scrub oaks and more open country.

17.2 Store.

23.2 Road to Drumm Valley.

24.7 Cafe, then turkey farm as you follow down a narrow valley.

25.7 Cross bridge: good road here and easier grades.

29.7 Road levels off as you pass through farms in this valley. Scattered homes.

34.2 Elderwood: store. State 201 goes right. Beyond here it is orchard country.

35.7 Left to Woodlake. Right takes you 15 miles to Visalia via short cut to State 216.

37.7 Woodlake outskirts.

39.0 Right 19 miles on State 216 to Visalia and airport: 58 miles.

TOUR 36

Lassen Peak is a splendid example of the volcanic cones that make up the eastern "Ring of Fire" that surrounds the Pacific Ocean. It was last active in 1914-21. Evidence of the eruption is still apparent. Snow remains year-round on the peak that is circled by a mountain road. Breathtaking beauty and vistas.

Location   North-central California.

Season   June through October. Summer is fine in the mountains, but getting there from the valley is arduous in the heat.

Transportation   Bus and airlines to Red Bluff.

Rating   Good roads all the way with long sections of biking shoulders. Light traffic. Easy grades mostly other than at Lassen on the climb up and when coming back: Shingletown to Manton. A moderate tour.

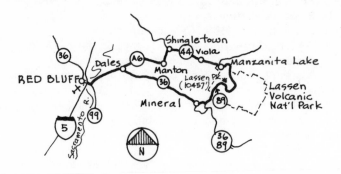

Tour Outline   124 miles, loop tour: 3 days, 2 nights.

Red Bluff is a large town with full services. Airport is on the south side of town. Tour begins east of town at

0.0   Junction of State 99/36. Go left on State 36, a 2-lane road through a rural area soon an open countryside setting. You start climbing a rise about the area. Vistas include the golden hills of ancient lava flows strewn with volcanic rock and dotted with oaks. Some patches of manzanita.

2.7   Mt. Shasta is apparent to the north on a clear day. Long grades here.

7.7   Long downhill into a valley and easy biking over short-rise hills. Some shade and a creek alongside the road; good for a refreshing splash if it's too hot.

10.7   Dales: store. State A6 goes left to Manton (return route). Road becomes more narrow after crossing Paynes Creek.

13.8   El. 1000 feet as you enter into green valley and scenic ride.

15.2   Trout farm, then start winding climb out of valley. Vistas of valley are very scenic.

17.7   Top rise in forest setting. Mt. Lassen in full view.

18.6 Store, cafe. Then a wider road: biking shoulder. Climbing easily out on a ridge with vistas.

19.7 El. 2000 feet.

22.2 Highway is cut through varied colored clays. Long grades.

24.2 Top rise to bike another ridge route. Vistas both sides.

25.6 El. 3000. Vistas of canyon on left.

28.0 Canyon view road.

29.3 Road goes to Lyonsville. State 36 narrows, winding and hilly through tall forest setting.

30.2 El. 4000 feet, then a vacant lodge.

32.5 After a downhill you pick up a wider road and easy grades.

34.7 Enter Lassen National Forest.

35.4 Campground, then come into a wide valley. At the end is

36.7 Mineral: full services. Out of town the road is very narrow as you climb through the tall forest, passing summer homes, creeks, open stretches of ferns and wildflowers.

38.4 El. 5000 feet, still climbing.

41.2 Left on State 89 to Lassen National Park. Grade up is easier now.

43.2 Top rise in sight of Mt. Lassen. Setting is more open and alpine.

45.4 Enter Lassen Volcanic National Park.

46.2 Entrance station. Campground here, also a chalet with food, gifts and rest rooms.

0.0 *Second day* continue up. For the next 7 miles it's one spectacular scene after another amongst high peaks, snows, lakes, bubbling cauldrons, multi-colored mud walls, waterfalls and alpine forests. At every turning there are vistas of the nearby mountains or the distant valleys and hills. Wildflowers blanket the hillside. This is tough biking.

1.4 El. 7000 feet.

3.6 Diamond Peak on left.

5.2 El. 8000 feet, then the very beautiful Emerald Lake, then keep climbing to

5.8 Lake Helen. Ground cover above here is mostly gravel with patches of snow and scattered trees. The pink cast to the snow is a micro-organism that flourishes on the snow when temperatures are right.

7.0 Top rise at about 8500 feet, then start a downhill as you swing away from mountain and go around behind it.

8.7   El. 8000 feet.

10.8   King Creek Picnic Area.

11.3   Very scenic meadow with creek flowing through it.

11.8   El. 7250 feet: Kings Creek. Beautiful setting. Vistas.

14.0   El. 7000 feet.

15.0   Summit Lake Campground. Tall forest now, and vistas are gone.

17.5   Devastated Area from the 1915 eruption of Lassen.

18.0   Exhibit. You can see where mud flows came from peak.

20.0   Hot Rock Exhibit.

22.0   Pass through open forest of ponderosa pine.

23.0   Climbing again.

25.0   Top rise to pass through Chaos Crags and Chaos Tumbles, another example of volcanic activity.

26.0   El. 6000 feet.

26.5   Manzanita Lake: Visitor Center, restaurant, lodge, store, campground with showers.

0.0   *Third day* leave campground and head down to

0.8   El 5000 feet.

1.0   Left on State 44 for Red Bluff. This is still a long downhill on a good road. Views behind include Lassen Peak through open forest and manzanita. Deer to be sighted here.

4.0   Leave Lassen National Forest.

7.2   Pass through community of Viola. Road grade down is easier now on a biking shoulder.

9.3   Rock Creek Road, then some short-rise hills.

11.0   Camp McCumber Road, then a biking shoulder.

13.8   Campground, then scattered homes in a more open area.

14.5   El. 4000 feet.

15.0   Rest area: toilets and water.

16.0   Bake shop.

17.0   Cafe and store.

17.8   Shingletown: cafe.

18.0   Left on road to Manton, a narrow, rough, winding, very hilly road leading through a shady forest and over ridges, then down to Manton. This is mostly downhill except at start. Forest grows right to the edge of the road. Very light traffic, but it winds so much that it's the kind of road you want to go down rather than up. The switchbacks take you down through manzanita, oaks, yellow grass and boulder strewn fields.

20.0 Views to left include ridge you biked up to Lassen Park.

21.0 Homes here.

22.0 Eeasier grades down.

23.0 Pass pond.

25.0 Cross one-lane bridge over Battle Creek, then right at intersection.

25.5 Cross Digger Creek and come into Manton: store and cafe.

25.8 Right on State A6. El. 2000 feet. Wider, better road without the bends and hills. Open countryside now.

26.5 Incredible junk shop!

32.2 Drop down to cross creek, climb up to an easy ride atop a mesa.

35.5 Downhill to

40.5 Dales. Right on State 36, 11 miles to start of tour: 51½ miles.

Russian Gulch.

TOUR 37

Sonoma County is the scene for most of this tour. It takes you north through the wine country to the Mendocino Coast and then south along the water's edge. Lots of pleasant surprises here at places like the Petrified Forest near Calistoga, the delightful Gowans Oak Tree where apple cider is offered on those hot summer days, and the shady ride through redwood forests.

Location   North of San Francisco.

Season   Year-round.

Rating   Generally the roads are good except around Calistoga. Traffic is mostly light and there are some sections with biking shoulders. The terrain is hilly to flat with some singular ups and downs on the beach and when crossing the ridge. An easy to moderate tour.

Tour Outline   225 miles, loop tour: 4 days, 3 nights.
The first day could be broken into 2 days.
    Santa Rosa is a large town with full services. The airport is north of town.

   0.0   Exit Sonoma County Airport to a right on Laughlin Road. You're in Russian River Valley country. Vineyards and orchards and scattered homes. Hills in the distance: golden grass with dark green oaks dotting the hills.

   0.7   Cross one-lane bridge.

   1.8   Left on River Road to Fulton, a wide road with a biking lane. Fruit stands.

   2.7   Cross intersection and keep ahead to cross freeway US 101 headed for Calistoga on the Mark West Springs Road through the hills in a narrow canyon. Traffic is light.

   5.3   Start climbing: scattered homes here.

   7.3   Narrow, winding, rough road as you follow stream through wooded canyons.

   8.6   Mark West Lodge, featuring French cuisine. You ride under a unique arbor covering the road. Beautiful gardens. Pick up Porter Creek Road here along stream. Short rise hills and easy biking.

  13.2   Left on Petrified Forest Road: light traffic on good road as you climb.

  14.0   Petrified Forest: fee. Excellent examples of petrified red-

woods and pine. The museum displays other petrified varieties of animal and plant life.

15.6 Drop into Napa Valley on very steep and winding downhill. Vistas of valley below.

17.0 Easier grade.

18.0 Left on State 128. To the right is Calistoga: full services. Great shops and eating places. Soaring center: instruction and rides. Mineral mud baths and hot springs.

On State 128 you travel north on a bumpy, narrow, concrete road through a valley of orchards and vineyards with golden hills all around. Homes scattered throughout this area. Traffic is light and you do have a strip of paving for biking which is smoother than the concrete.

20.0 Climb out of valley into woods. Shady ride.

21.0 Top rise. Sonoma County line and a better road.

22.0 Bridge: easier grade down as you come into open valley and vineyards.

23.7 Good example of a stone fence made from the volcanic rocks strewn over these fields.

27.0 Hilly, winding road through wooded canyon into next valley. Stream beside you. Scenic.

29.0 Climb away from creek on easy grade to vistas of hills.

30.0 Road to Santa Rosa goes left.

31.0 Concrete road: biking shoulder. Vineyards and orchards. Some small wineries along here.

33.4 Store.

33.5 Store; still easy biking in a valley growing fruit and nuts of many varieties. Better road.

35.5 On a bend a road goes to Geyser, a route that comes back to State 128 farther north.

39.0 Cross Russian River: toilets here. Then come into Geyserville: full services along here and north to Cloverdale.

39.8 Right on US 101, a busy road with a biking shoulder. To your right are the hills on other side of the Russian River. Wineries and scattered homes.

41.0 Campground.

42.6 Four lane road.

42.8 Take Asti Road, paralleling freeway. Short rise hills; easy biking.

44.7 Campground down School House Road.

45.0 Asti: store and cafe, then Asti Winery. Visitors welcome. Keep ahead on paralleling road.

46.2 Road to Santa Rosa.

47.0 Freeway ends and you join it going right. Biking shoulder into Cloverdale: full services. Road is very busy as you pass through town.

49.5 Climb out of town.

49.8 Left on State 128 and drop down into a valley. Light traffic as you take a couple of short-rise hills then start a steady climb through a winding canyon road with switchbacks. The climb gets steeper; some bike and hike here.

54.0 Top rise: vistas. Then short-rise hills. Orchards and vineyards up here.

56.5 County 111 goes right to Hopland and Ukiah.

57.4 Start downhill; still a winding route.

58.8 Level off; stream on left.

63.0 Elkhorn Road, come into Yorkville: cafe.

64.0 Cafe and camping on a hilltop.

67.5 Canyon ride alongside Navarro River.

67.7 Road goes left to Anchor Bay. On the other side of the river is a evergreen forest, while this side remains golden hills and oaks.

72.3 Top rise and start long downhill.

73.5 Cross Robinson Creek onto flat area into Anderson Valley.

74.5 State 253 goes right then come into Boonville: full services. County fairgrounds.

75.5 Road goes left to Manchester. Outside of town there is a road, Anderson Valley Way, which will take you through the area and rejoin State 128. State 128 has a biking shoulder. Cool riding as you begin to feel the ocean breezes coming up the valley from the coast.

78.5 Anderson Valley Way goes left. Lose biking shoulders.

80.0 Cross Indian Creek and come into Philo: store, cafe, motel. End of day for motelers

82.0 Store and laundromat.

82.8 Gowans Oak Tree, a vegetable and fruit stand that has a specialty of apple cider. A delightful drink! Toilets and picnic area here.

83.4 Hardy Woods State Park: camping, swimming.

0.0 *Second day* continue north on State 128, easy biking.

4.0 Store.

5.6 Navarro: cafe and store. Beyond here you are into the deep redwood forest, a very scenic route with lots of spots for camping and picnicking alongside the Navarro River. Forest exhibit by industry explaining how forests are developed, maintained and harvested. Rest rooms. This is all downhill in the shade of giant redwoods.

12.0 Paul M. Dimmick State Park: camping.

14.0 Sign: High Water Mark of December 1964, about 10 feet above road!

18.6 Alongside the tidal Navarro River. Country is more open now.

19.6 Left on State 1 over a bridge across the Navarro River, climbing steeply on a biking shoulder. Great vistas of Pacific Ocean.

20.3 Top rise. This coast road to Anchor Bay is a series of ups and downs over headlands and down into inlets: some bike and hike. The scenery is very dramatic as the road hugs the coast most of the way. To your left is the coast range, while the shoreline is mostly grassy bluffs and headlands that stick out into the water. Rocky islands and bird roosts are everywhere. Extensive cattle and sheep grazing on the coast along with dairy farming. The towns are small and accommodations simple. In spring and early summer wildflowers cover the hills. At several points near towns there are other roads that lead down closer to the water. You take your chances: some are dead end. Traffic is light and the road generally good with some sections of biking shoulder.

21.0 Loose biking shoulder. Note the extensive use of wood fences and their different designs.

25.2 Elk, named for now extinct elk that once roamed here: food and lodgings. Beyond here you can go down under Greenwood Creek to the beach.

27.0 Campground.

34.0 Irish Beach: a community of expensive beach homes.

36.0 Cross Alder Creek and swing away from the ocean.

37.0 Manchester Beach State Park: camping. Also a KOA Campground. Then come into Manchester: store, shops.

40.0 Cross Garcia River: lighthouse at mouth of river.

41.3 Campground and road to lighthouse. Because of the climatic conditions caused by the land masses, wind currents, and warm water close to the land, you have less fog and cold weather here.

42.0 Point Arena: full services. This is the closest point on the American coast to Hawaii.

45.3 Cross Mote Creek.

46.6 Cross Schooner Gulch and bike along water again.

49.0 Forest is between you and water now as you pass scattered homes and come into Anchor Bay.

52.7 Motel. End of day for motelers or go on 3½ miles to motel in Gualala.

53.0 Anchor Bay Campgrounds: showers.

0.0 *Third day* continue south to

0.3 Anchor Bay: store, cafe, laundromat.

2.2 Enter Gualala: cafe, motel, stores, Playhouse Theater.

4.0 Campground. Beyond Gualala the route is much less hilly. There are few inlets to cross and the road is mostly easy biking. Soon you will be passing Sea Ranch for several miles. Appreciators of architecture will enjoy this section. Most of the homes are different and enjoy a singularity on these grassy bluffs. There are roads amongst these expensive homes for a closer look.

11.0 Road to Annapolis.

12.0 Sea Ranch Lodge, store and restaurant.

14.5 Road to Healdsburg as you pass through Stewarts Point.

19.3 Kruse-Rhododendron State Park to left up a dirt road. Hills beyond here.

22.0 Salt Point State Park: camping. Wooded ride here.

23.7 Motel and restaurant in a small community.

26.0 Timber Cove Inn: restaurant, hotel and shop. A very imposing structure looking down on a cove.

27.0 Fort Ross: store.

28.0 Biking shoulder. Easy going as you come to

28.5 Fort Ross State Park: exhibit of fort and blockhouse.

30.0 Beyond state park there is a really steep climb, 2 miles long up to breathtaking views of shoreline and ocean. This is the steepest climb you will make and it's always next to the cliffs. One mistake and it's a long way down!

32.0 Top rise; and then a switchback drop to

36.5 Cross Russian Gulch into Jenner.

39.0 Restaurants, cabins as you bike alongside Russian River inlet. Scattered homes with services for touring bikers.

40.5 State 116 goes left, then cross Russian River: restaurants, cabins, store and campground here. Beyond here there are several Sonoma Beach State Parks for day use.

43.7 Wrights Beach State Park: camping on water.

44.7 Gleason Beach State Park: look for leopard seals down

on rocks here. Access to beach here. Vista point also overlooking a small line of homes perched atop the cliffs.

45.4 Portugese Beach and Schoolhouse Beach State Park both have toilets. Scattered homes here as you come to Salmon Creek Beach: toilets. Lagoon here alongside the town of Ocean View.

48.7 Cross Salmon Creek and climb up and over to

49.5 Bodega Bay: full services. This is a large beach town with a good harbor for many recreation and commercial boats. The town's most recent claim to fame is its use for the Alfred Hitchcock film, THE BIRDS, a very bad film.

0.0 *Fourth day* continue south and beyond the town you move inland between the hills. Some long grades here.

8.0 Left on road to Occidental: the Valley Ford-Firestone Road. This is a hard one to notice. Ahead on State 1 is Valley Ford with cafe and store. This is a narrow rough road with an easy grade up to a right on the Bodega Highway for Sebastopol. Light traffic on this easy road through Firestone; store. Climb up and away from town to

12.5 Top rise. Vistas of valley ahead: orchards, vineyards and surrounding hills.

14.0 Fruit stand. Biking on bumpy concrete road.

15.7 Come into Sebastopol: full services.

17.0 Left on State 116 to Forestville, and leave town on a wide road: biking shoulder. Orchards and vineyards. Fruit stands. Some services along the route: stores and cafes.

19.3 Road to Occidental goes left.

20.2 Road to Graton goes left.

21.5 Winery: visitors welcome. Steep hills now as you come to Forestville.

22.0 Enter Forestville: store, cafe

23.5 Right on road to Rio Nido: light traffic. Forestville Youth Park just outside of town has toilets and water.

25.0 Right to Fulton on riverside road. Campground here with canoes to rent for boating the Russian River which you are now following upstream. This is a very good road: biking shoulder. Easy biking.

25.5 Road goes left to Healdsburg. Vistas of countryside along here as you bike through orchards and vineyards.

30.7 Left on Laughlin Road on signs to County Airport.

31.8 Cross one-lane bridge.
39.5 Airport and end of tour.

Desert biking on wide roads.

NEW MEXICO

The Spanish settled in New Mexico before the Pilgrims even thought of coming to America. Towns like Santa Fe were established long before the first permanent English colony settled in Jamestown, Virginia. When once it was a search for gold and silver that brought men here, now it is the good weather, cool high altitudes and scenic splendor of vast deserts, mesas and rugged mountains.

Bike touring can be good fun here. The roads are often very wide and lightly traveled. The grades are generally easy but long, and the climate very agreeable with much of the state above a mile high. Albuquerque, Santa Fe and Taos are exciting fun places where the cultures of Indians and Spanish flavor the charm of these cities.

Visitors to New Mexico can write for more information from the Tourist Division, New Mexico Department of Development, 113 Washington Avenue, Santa Fe, New Mexico 87501.

TOUR 38

Southwest desert country is the scene for this tour that loops north from Farmington into Colorado and back south. A visit to Mesa Verde is the main feature of the trip. The contrast between desert biking and then biking in sight of snow-patched mountains is exciting. A side diversion could include a day stopover in Durango with a scenic ride north through the San Juan Mountains to Silverton. For more information write Agent, Rio Grande Depot, Durango, Colorado 81301.

Location   Northwest New Mexico.

Season   Spring, summer, fall. Summer temperatures are comfortable at these altitudes.

Transportation   Bus and airlines to Farmington.

Rating   Generally light traffic on good roads with easy but long grades. Some stiff climbing at Mesa Verde. This is a moderate tour.

Reference   Write for map-brochure, Superintendent, Mesa Verde National Park, Colorado 81330.

Tour Outline   157 miles: 4 days, 3 nights.
An extra day can easily be added for a stay at Mesa Verde.
    Farmington is a large town with full services. The airport is in town.

0.0 Exit Farmington Municipal Airport overlooking the city and San Juan Basin. Use Municipal Airport Drive for town. Motels along this road as you drop down to a

1.0 Right on US 550 (Main Street). Left takes you to downtown Farmington. Leave town through a commercial/industrial area. Some scattered homes as you ride a road with lots of room for biking. Traffic is moderate. You are in the San Juan Basin flanked by mesas. Large farms here beside the San Juan River.

3.0 State 170 goes right. (State 140 from Colorado.) Climbing here to rise above valley.

4.0 Top mesa. Shiprock (7178) is visible in distance. This prominent rock formation juts up 1600 feet from desert floor. For some it represented a schooner. Then drop down into valley again. Great vistas here of the desert and its yellow mud hills.

7.3 Store as you pass by Kirkland.

9.0 Cafe-store, laundromat, then restaurant.

11.0 Fruitland road.

12.5 Working coal mine.

14.0 Store.

15.0 Pass through Waterflow. Road is rough, and narrow beyond here.

16.0 Store.

18.2 Store.

19.0 Interesting rock formation.

21.5 Leave mesas behind. To the right are views of mountains in Colorado.

24.0 Shiprock is reddish in morning sunlight. Very impressive. About 15 miles away. Then come alongside yellow mud dunes and mesas.

26.0 Store, laundromat, cafe, campground as you come into Shiprock under a shady route. Shiprock has full services.

27.0 Right on US 666 for Cortez and start climbing. Good

vistas behind of Shiprock and desert. Road is narrow with broken edges. Light traffic with big trucks.

28.5 Top rise. Ahead are the LaPlata Mountains in Colorado. Around you is the same yellow desert mud, mesas and rock outcroppings, sparsely covered with grasses and sage.

30.0 More good vistas of Shiprock.

36.5 Good road with room for biking. Long grades, difficult only in their length.

38.5 Top mesa: microwave tower on left. Excellent vistas of desert behind and below. Road swings right ahead, between mesas and mountains as you

41.5 Cross into Colorado riding through Ute Mountain Indian Reservation. Some solitary rock formations jut up a few hundred feet from desert floor. Very colorful.

43.5 Mancos River, then store.

47.5 US 160 comes in from left and the point where 4 states meet. Gas station here. You are in a long steady climb to a great plateau stretching north to Grand Junction.

55.5 Towaoc: behind is Hermano Peak (9500).

56.7 Stores here as you leave Indian Reservation and move onto the rich farmlands and grazing lands flanked by mountains and mesa walls. Easy biking now with cool temperatures.

60.0 Cortez ahead on plateau, LaPlata Mountains ahead on right.

61.0 Store and cafe.

62.5 Campground.

63.5 Come into Cortez through industrial/commercial area.

64.5 Cortez city limits (6200). Cortez has full services with many campgrounds and motels on this end of town.

0.0 *Second day* start tour at junction of US 666/160. Go right on US 160 to Durango.

1.7 Chamber of Commerce at east end of town. Leave town on 2-lane road with biking shoulder, riding through the mountains. Light traffic. Very scenic.

3.2 Campground and store. The mesas viewed here are dark with trees.

8.7 Rest area: water and toilets.

10.4 Entrance to Mesa Verde National Park: campgrounds and stores here at entrance. The ride up to the mesa is a tough one, 6954 to 8572 feet at Park Point; 10 miles. From the entrance to the ruins at Balcony House is another 16 miles. The museum, Visitor Center and guided tours are excellent aids to understanding these ruins and the cliff dwellers who once lived here. Within the park there are full services, including camping.

0.0 *Third day* leave the park and head for Durango.

0.8 Campground, then a big downhill. Beautiful vistas here of mountain country: open fields, scattered homes.

5.8 Road to Mancos: food and lodgings.

6.5 Campground, store and laundromat.

7.3 Cross State 184. Services here.

7.8 Cross Mancos River, climbing steadily.

8.8 Campground and cafe.

10.8 Uphill climb stiffens.

12.3 Top rise, then some ups and downs as you pass alongside the LaPlata Mountains. Hesperus Peak, el. 13,225 feet.

13.8 Campground. Beyond here loose biking shoulder.

16.3 Wide shoulder for biking on new section of road that climbs easily, then steeply through a pass.

20.8 Top rise, and start down.

22.3 Pass ski area, then campground, motel.

23.0 State 140 goes right to Farmington, a shortcut. Along here you can see the land stretching down and away to the desert and Farmington.

23.8 Start long downhill. Very fast as you head for Durango and a desert setting.

27.8 Enter narrow canyon.

31.3 Motel.

31.8 Motel and cafe, and campground.

32.3 Campground, then motel and more services as you come into Durango.

32.8 Campground.

32.9 Cross Animas River.

33.1 Right on US 550 and come into Durango: full services. Visit here on Main Street or take a railroad ride to Silverton.

0.0 *Fourth day* take US 550 to leave town alongside the Animas River Valley.

1.5 Cafe, then restaurant as you pass through a narrow canyon with the river.

4.0 Right on US 550, climbing stiffly up above the Animas River to a mesa. Vistas of river and valley below. Light traffic here as you have easy biking atop the mesa. Green farmlands and grazing fields. Scattered homes as you run out on a long finger with dropoffs both sides. This is mostly downhill to Farmington.

10.0 Campground and cafe. Then start to drop down off mesa to the Animas River Valley. Beautiful vistas of country before you.

16.0 Cross Animas River as you pass through Bondad: store.

17.5 Store.

18.5 Store.

19.5 Enter New Mexico: wide biking shoulder along edge of the Animas River Valley, overlooking farms and countryside.

24.0 Cedar Hill: store.

24.2 Cross Animas River.

32.0 Divided highway as you come into Aztec: full services.

33.2 State 44 goes left to downtown Aztec.

33.8 Cross Animas River. A right turn here leads 1 mile to Aztec Ruins National Monument. Very fine example of pueblo ruins and restoration. One pueblo covers two acres, stands three stories and contained 500 rooms.

34.0 Camping. The road from here to Farmington is 4-laned with a median. Many services scattered along here. Traffic is moderate.

38.2 Pass through Flora Vista: cafe.

39.2 Store.

41.5 Motel, cafe, then come into Farmington in the San Juan Basin where the Animas River joins the San Juan River. Farmington has full services.

47.3 Airport Drive, one mile to airport: 48½ miles.

OREGON

The state of Oregon welcomes you for a visit, but don't remain! This is the first state in the nation that has a policy of encouraging visitors while discouraging immigrants. It's easy to see why they want to preserve what there is for those already there. This is a wonderful land that combines the very best in seashore, mountains and desert.

Four hundred miles of rugged seashore offers everything in the way of beach exploring, nature study and fishing. Giants like Mount Hood (11,235), Mount Jefferson (10,495) and the Three Sisters dominate the snow-patched Cascade ridge. Excellent hiking in this region. In the broad valleys between the coast and mountains there are great whitewater routes, vast farmlands, forests and a good network of roads to get you "into Oregon".

For more information about visiting Oregon write to Oregon State Highway Division, Travel Information, 101 State Highway Building, Salem, Oregon 97310.

Crater Lake.

TOUR 39

Touring north of Klamath to Crater Lake is a delight. Excellent roads and quiet, scenic splendor are enjoyed as you skirt the basin country and move up into the foothills around the dome. You will gain about 3,000 feet in 70 miles, but it doesn't hurt! Viewing the magnificent blue Crater Lake makes it all worth the effort.

Location   South-central Oregon.

Season   Mid-June through September.

Transportation   Buses and airlines to Klamath Falls.

Rating   Excellent roads with biking shoulders most of the route. Easy grades other than at Crater Lake. Light traffic all the way. This is an easy to moderate tour.

Reference   Write for map-brochure Superintendent, Crater Lake National Park, Oregon 97604.

Tour Outline   175 miles, loop tour: 3 days, 2 nights.
Klamath Falls is a large town with full services. The airport is on the south side of town.

 0.0 Exit Klamath Falls Municipal Airport next to Kingsley Field Air Force Base. At airport entrance go left on Joe Wright Road. Countryside is open basin stretching north for miles: ranches and scattered homes. Views of Mt. Shasta to the south over the hills. The Klamath River irrigates the area. Light traffic. Look for white pelicans.
 1.8 Stop, then continue ahead.
 2.8 Right on US 97 a busy road with a biking shoulder.
 3.3 Cross Klamath River.
 4.0 4-lane road, then go right to State 140, west to Keno and Medford. Left under US 97, and then
 4.8 Right on State 140, an excellent road with lots of room for biking. Rise above homes. Light traffic.
 5.6 Level off: 2-lane road with biking shoulder. Vistas of yellow hills and scattered oaks. Long grades passing through forest and farmlands. Pine smells good on a hot summer day. Scenic ride.
10.4 Lakeshore Drive and Moore Park Road.
10.8 Loose biking shoulder: good road.
13.2 Drop down to bike alongside Upper Klamath Lake. Very

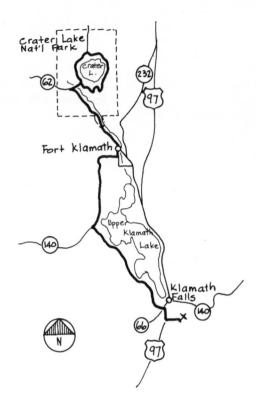

scenic area as you skirt the lake and its marshes in a vast basin stretching north to Crater Lake.

14.2 Cross bridge and then your right at lakeshore. Forest rises on hills at your left. Lots of access to water.

15.7 Rest area: toilets.

16.3 Steep climb away from lake. Vistas behind.

17.0 Top rise, then another rise through the tall forest. Very scenic area.

18.0 Top rise, then another rise.

18.6 Top rise, level off, then a long downhill to lake again.

21.0 Level ride again through grazing lands. Lake in distance.

24.5 Enter Winema National Forest: biking shoulder.

25.3 Vicinity map on board.

26.7 Restaurant, store.

27.8 Right on road to Rocky Point and Fort Klamath. Restaurant and cabins here. Road is narrow and winding through a resort area with scattered homes bordering the Upper Klamath National Wildlife Refuge. Light traffic on some short rise hills.

30.0 Fork: keep left and climb up through the forest from lake to a very wide highway. Good vistas.

32.0 Top rise and continue along lake. Open forest setting.

34.2 Drop down alongside lake again: marshes.

37.0 Rest area: toilets. Leave lake here. Remote area along here as you ride above basin and grazing lands.

42.0 Cross Three-Mile Creek.

43.5 Leave Winema National Forest and turn out onto prairie grazing lands.

44.2 Loose biking shoulder; road narrows. Peak of Crater Lake visible on left: Mt. Scott (8926).

48.0 Left to Fort Klamath and Crater Lake.

49.8 Stop: keep ahead on State 62 for Crater Lake. State 62 goes right. In Fort Klamath there is a store, cafe, motels and campgrounds. Leave town on a narrow, rough road with light traffic, easy biking on level ride. This area will make an excellent alternate overnight stop if you cannot make the Park.

52.4 National Park exhibit about "the mountain that isn't there".

54.3 Cabins and camping.

55.2 Motel and store.

55.3 Winema National Forest.

56.0 Crater Lake National Park: good wide road through tall forest. Start climbing on easy grades alongside Annie Creek in its canyon.

64.4 Overlook.

65.3 Right to Crater Lake and entrance station at 6,200 feet. Campground here at entrance. Then cross Annie Creek.

66.7 Cross Goodbye Creek then start climbing.

69.0 Park Headquarters. Left to Rim Village on a very steep climb up with switchbacks. Patches of snow here in July.

71.2 Top rise.

71.8 Road to Bend and Eugene. This is the first part of the Rim Drive.

72.0 Rim Village: store, cafe, lodge. End first day. Vistas here of the lake. 72 miles.

0.0 *Second day* start one-way tour of Crater Lake. This is a tough tour made up of a series of long ups and downs. However there are many view points for stopping, several rest rooms, one-way light traffic and generally a good road for biking. It is 31 miles around the loop and a whole day can be spent here; take a lunch. Or better still plan to take the boat trip on the lake. The setting is a mix of open hills falling away from the crater; forests, gravel fields and snow-patched peaks in the distance. The best time to view the lake is at midday when the sun gives the water its full color.

3.7 Start one-way drive. Look for tiny wildflowers, hardly noticeable close to the ground.

5.6 Road comes in from Bend.

8.0 Rest area: toilets.

10.0 Parking for lake tours: toilets.

16.0 Picnic grounds: toilets. Mt. Scott (8926) on your left.

16.2 Road to Cloudcap: vista.

17.0 Vistas of Upper Klamath Lake and basin.

18.0 Rest area: toilets. Road goes to Lost Creek Campground. Do not plan to take this road through to State 232: road closed.

20.7 Drinking water coming out of mountainside. Vistas along here of Upper Klamath Lake and basin.

25.0 Nature Trail down to Lost Creek Campground.

28.0 Park Headquarters. Right takes you 3 miles back up to Rim Village and camp. 31 miles.

Third day head back the way you came, 22 miles to Fort Klamath. A left here on State 62 will get you to Klamath Falls (45 miles), but the road is more narrow, rougher, not nearly as scenic, and much busier than the first day route. So keep ahead and use the same route (50 miles) back to the airport. It's just as delightful on the return trip. 72 miles.

Three Arch Rocks.

TOUR 40

Many miles of this tour are on traffic-free roads in the backwoods country west of Portland. Delightful scenery. When you come out on the coast road, it's to visit a number of small towns. Don't pass up the opportunity to see the Tillamook Cheese Factory, go beachcombing for glass floats, or enjoy some of the fine seafoods of the area.

Location   Northwest Oregon.

Season   Year-round. Be prepared for cold wet days along coast.

Transportation   Buses, rail and airlines to Portland.

Rating   Good roads, not too many tough grades and light traffic, except along US 101. This is a moderate tour.

Tour Outline   193 miles: 4 days, 3 nights.
Start tour west of Portland at Glenwood, a small community.

0.0 Junction State 6 and road to Timber. Gas station here; make arrangements for parking. Head for Timber on a narrow, winding bumpy road through the forest. Scattered farms and homes along this mostly wooded route. Very scenic valley section. Grass grows right to edge of road.

4.0 Start switchbacks out of valley.

5.0 Top rise and come alongside RR tracks to climb to

5.7 Top rise and start down through woods.

6.0 Timber. Cross RR tracks. Cafe. Keep ahead for Veronia, climbing on easy grade to ridge ride in woods. Scattered homes.

8.0 Start long downhill to

9.0 Cross US 26: cafe, store. One more hill, then easy biking on mostly downhill run as you pass down the valley of the Nehalem River which you will cross many times. This is very pleasant biking through woods and farmlands. Look for deer.

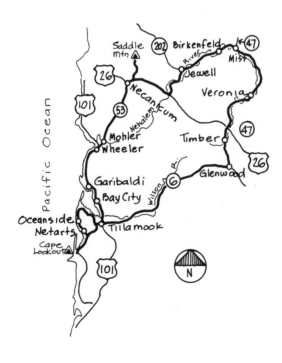

14.0   Cross Nehalem River.
16.5   Cross Nehalem River.
17.8   Coffee shop at golf club.
18.5   Village.
19.0   Join State 47 for Veronia. Shoulder for biking on this moderately busy highway.
19.5   Cross Nehalem River and come into Veronia: full services.
21.4   County Museum in town. Then climb out of town through residential area.
21.8   Cross Nehalem River and go left. Stores here. Road beyond here is a level valley road through big farms. Scattered homes, light traffic.
23.5   Cross Nehalem River, then onto a winding valley road.
25.2   Cross Nehalem River.
25.5   Cafe at Pittsburgh. Cross Nehalem River again and go left at a fork in road for Mist. Easy biking alongside river. Access here for swimming or picnicking.
28.5   County Park: camping.

 0.0   *Second day* continue on State 47 for Mist.
 1.0   Fork in road: keep on State 47 for Mist. Then some short rise hills.
 4.0   Mist Cedar and Shake Company.
 7.7   Mist: go left on State 202; biking shoulder. State 47 goes right.
10.0   Cross Nehalem River.
12.5   Berkenfeld: cafe, store. Hills beyond here.
13.0   Cross Nehalem River.
14.8   Cross Nehalem River.
18.2   Cross Nehalem River.
21.0   Cross Nehalem River.
23.2   Cross Nehalem River.
23.8   Come into Jewell after crossing Beneke Creek: tavern here. Go left on road to Elsie and US 26, following Nehalem River downstream. Scenic.
28.5   Cross Nehalem River.
29.7   Very big log!
32.2   Pass under bridge and come up to US 26. Go left across bridge, to the right about one-half mile is a cafe and motel. Stiff climb up from bridge on biking shoulder.

35.0 Elsie: store, cafe. Long grades here.

38.0 Start stiff climb.

40.5 Top rise and then a very long downhill on excellent 4-lane road with shoulder for biking.

43.5 Saddle Mountain State Park: camping. Take this very scenic road in 7 miles to park. A stiff uphill, then downhill, then up again. But it's worth it. Good chance of seeing elk and deer here in this tall Tillamook State Forest. Just a beautiful ride in a rain forest setting. Stumps of the virgin forest logged off years ago. 50½ miles.

Third day take the 7 mile road back to US 26 and a

0.0 Right on US 26 to go downhill passing a drive-in eating place before coming to a

0.7 Left on State 53 at Necanicum: cafe. State 53 is a hilly, winding, narrow road through the forest.

3.5 Top rise and start down winding through logged areas.

5.7 Road straightens; keep on down through forest.

6.8 Cross bridge over North Fork Nehalem River, then into a valley with farms and scattered homes. Scenic.

7.8 Cross North Fork Nehalem River. Salmon hatchery just beyond here: open to visitors.

13.4 Cross Rack Heap Creek and enter into a broad valley with large farms.

16.0 Road goes right to Nehalem.

17.4 Cabins and cafe as you cross Nehalem River and come into Mohler: store.

18.7 Left on US 101, skirting tidal marshes of Nehalem Bay. Vistas of Pacific Ocean. Moderate traffic.

19.2 Wheeler: motels, cafe, stores. Then keep biking along river's edge where the Nehalem River is separated from the ocean by a sandspit. Short rise hills.

24.6 Good road with biking shoulder. Then a long stretch of services including campgrounds, as you pass through Manhattan Beach, Lake Lytle, Rockaway, Bayview, Garibaldi, Bay City. Some other shore roads are closer to the water. Some are worth investigating. Most come back to US 101 within a few blocks. Great vistas of ocean. Some green wooded sections between the seaside towns.

32.7 Cross Miami River.

38.3 Cross Kilchis River.

39.2 Tillamook Cheese Factory: visitors welcome.

40.5 Enter into Tillamook: full services. In town follow signs to visitor center and museum. Then take road west on 3rd Street out of town to Cape Meares and Oceanside, traveling through the "richest dairyland in the world".

42.6 Cross Tillamook River and go right on the Cape Meares Road, a narrow road following the shoreline of the estuary. Hills rise on left. Traffic is light as you pass scattered homes.

44.0 Public Boat Landing: toilets.

47.6 Round headland to reach artificially created Meares Lake. Fish for rainbow and cutthroat here next to the ocean!

47.8 Left on road to lighthouse and Oceanside, climbing steeply through scenic forest.

49.0 Top rise.

49.8 Right into Camp Meares State Park. View the Three Arches Rocks with sea lions and birds. Also check out the octopus tree, and the old lighthouse below the parking area. Big ups and downs beyond here.

52.0 Oceanside: good views of the Three Arches Rocks from the public beach. Then a stiff climb up and then down to

53.8 Netarts: full services here in this very small beach town. End of day for motelers. 61 miles.

54.3 Right on road to Cape Lookout State Park, skirting Netarts Bay. Across the water is a sandspit which is also part of the park.

55.8 Road goes left 6 miles to Tillamook.

56.8 Wee Willie's: quality food and baked goods. Be sure to eat here, either supper or breakfast. A very interesting gift shop next door features work of local artists and craftsmen.

58.8 Store and camping on the water: toilets.

59.3 Fork: keep left into Cape Lookout State Park.

59.8 Campground. End of day: 67 miles.

 0.0 *Fourth day* take road back to

 4.0 Right on road to Tillamook, climbing away from the water into the forest.

 5.3 Road goes left to beach, then top rise to bike on short rise hills through some woods, farms and scattered homes.

7.4 Campground.

8.3 Rejoin road from Tillamook. Left to Cape Meares. Keep ahead for Tillamook. Go straight through town on State 6. Leave town on a 4-lane road.

10.6 2-lane road: biking shoulder. Open country and steady grade up to hills ahead.

14.0 Enter into the hills as you follow up along the Wilson River which you will cross many times before reaching the top. Many accesses to river for swimming or picnicking. You will be biking through the Tillamook Burn Area: 355,000 acres lost in 1933.

14.4 Campground.

17.0 Narrow road: no shoulder.

17.6 Store and smokehouse, cafe.

18.3 Tillamook State Forest; still an easy grade.

26.6 Forest campground.

27.0 Inn and cafe.

31.3 Forest campground, then a rest area: toilets.

32.3 Store and cafe.

36.2 Biking shoulder as you enter into a slide area.

37.6 Waterfall on right.

39.8 Rest area: water and toilets.

41.0 Top rise and start fast down. Views of Mt. St. Helens straight ahead.

43.0 Forest campground.

44.3 Easier grade down.

45.3 Cross Gales Creek: campground.

46.6 Glenwood and junction of road to Timber. End of tour.

WASHINGTON

If any state can rival California for the title of "the biking state" it is Washington. The population here is into biking for racing, touring, transportation and just plain fun in local neighborhoods. The interest here is apparent, as indicated by over one dozen clubs existing in the Seattle area.

For the touring biker there are endless opportunities to explore the state, its natural wonders and historic sites. The coastal region beckons visitors to the rain forests and surf. The Cascades offer alpine splendor to those bikers who will put out the effort. And

Coastal valley on Olympic Peninsula.

the eastern desert and canyon country recalls the days of western expansion along the Snake River and the mighty Columbia.

Of interest to bikers here and nationwide is a periodical published in Seattle. While the emphasis is on local biking in the state, it does cover many subjects of interest to all bikers. This is a great magazine for tips, how-to information, where-to for touring, racing results, etc. Get *The Bicycle Paper,* P.O. Box 842, Seattle, Washington 98111. Bi-monthly, $2.25 postpaid.

Books about biking in Washington are, *Bicycling Backroads Around Puget Sound,* by Erin and Bill Woods. An excellent detailed description of 54 tours, mostly east of Puget Sound. Maps and sketches. And *Bicycling in Seattle,* by Steward. Also of interest to cyclists in the area is a book, *Exploring by Bicycle: Southwest British Columbia, Northwest Washington,* by Willson. This book describes in detail 24 tours. Maps and photos.

Visitors wanting information about the state should write Tourist Promotion, Department of Commerce and Economic Development, General Administration Bldg., Olympic, Washington 98504.

TOUR 41

Looping around Mt. Rainier is an exciting road adventure. If the weather cooperates there are magnificent views of Mt. Rainier on most of your tour.

Location   Central Washington.

Season   June through October. Summer weekends are busy, but it's still worth it to go then.

Rating   Roads are generally good and traffic is light. In the park speed limits help control the car drivers. There are two major climbs and descents, both about 2,700 feet. This is a difficult tour.

Reference   Write for map-brochure, Superintendent, Mount Rainier National Park, Longmire, Washington 98397.

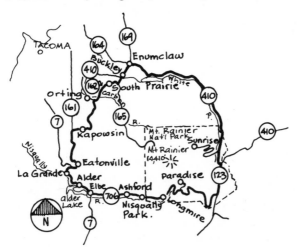

Tour Outline   148 miles, loop tour: 3 days, 2 nights.
An extra day can be added by taking the road up to Sunrise and incomparable views of Mt. Rainier. Include some hiking here.

Start tour in Enumclaw, a small town with full services: bike shop. In downtown section at junction of State 164 and 164Y (Cole Street)

0.0 Take State 164Y south out of town to join,

0.3 State 410 to Buckley and Tacoma. 2-lane road with shoulder for biking in heavy traffic. The area is mostly open with a rural/residential setting. To your left the snowy Cascades dominate the horizon. The mass of Mt. Rainier is visible in good weather.

2.5 Cross White River, named so because of the glacier dust it carries from the grinding glaciers atop Mt. Rainier. Then come into Buckley: full services.

3.7 Left on State 165; narrow shoulder for biking.

5.2 Right on State 162, (State 165 goes up behind Mt. Rainier to Mowich Lake) a narrow rough concrete road; easy biking. Traffic is light. Setting is mostly wooded.

6.7 Open valley with farms and scattered homes.

7.2 After fork cross bridge as you pass through South Prairie. Very easy biking beyond here on a seldom used road; grass growing in road cracks.

11.6 Cross Carbon River, and then pass by Nelco, a plant.

13.7 Left to Electron on Orville Road; wide road with light traffic. Easy biking by saw mills, scattered homes, farms. Ridge on left.

16.0 Winding road.

17.0 Right and over bridge to cross Puyallup River and start climbing in wooded setting.

18.5 McDonald Road goes right. Pleasant biking through woods.

20.7 Entrance to St. Regis Paper Company on a right bend.

21.2 Kapowsin Lake.

22.2 Cross RR tracks and enter Kapowsin; store. Rural community. Light traffic.

25.4 Left on State 161; store, cafe. Easy biking on long grades.

28.0 Stiff climb.

29.0 Top rise at Clear Lake: resort area, camping.

29.7 Vistas, and then open country. Short rise hills and downhill to pass

32.0 Restaurant, then reach

34.0 Start of uphill to Eatonville: full services. Narrow concrete road out of here with paved shoulder.

35.5 Cross Mashelle River.

36.2 Cross Little Mashelle River; biking through an area of mixed farms and woods.

37.0 Left on State 706; wide shoulder for biking. Climb through forest area into

38.0 La Grande: store. Then a stiff climb winding up above Alder Lake and Dam. Ugly signs of clear cutting on nearby mountains.

38.4 Motel, then good biking once you top rise. Vistas of mountains and Nisqually River below.

41.3 Rest area overlooking Alder Dam. Then a downhill to Alder; store. Level road with shoulder for biking as you pass around Alder Lake.

43.0 Access to Alder Lake; toilets.

47.0 Come into Elbe: cafe and store.

47.7 Left on State 706. State 7 goes right. Same good road with biking shoulder.

51.7 Easy going. Look for deer here in open forest.

53.0 Rest area.

53.4 Cross RR tracks onto bumpy concrete road.

54.5 Ashford: store with laundromat and hot showers.

56.0 Motel.

58.0 Beautiful open forest with ferns, grasses and wildflowers.

58.2 Cabins, trailers and camping. Then cross Copper Creek to restaurant. Nisqually River on right.

59.3 Restaurant. Across the street is a steam engine exhibit and a small logging operation.

59.7 Cedar Park Ranch: cabins and camping.

60.3 Motel, then Nisqually Park and Gateway Motel; cafe. There is also an AYH Hostel in this area. End of first day. 60 miles.

0.0 *Second day* head for park and

1.0 Enter Mount Rainier National Park (2003). Fee. Heavy forest ride on a good road. Traffic is moderate but generally slow. You start climbing easily on a shady, winding route.

1.3 Sunshine Point Campground.

2.0 Keep on road to Longmire and Paradise.

4.2 Vista of Mount Rainier at Kantz Mudflow Overlook. Then start the stiff climb up alongside Nisqually River and overlooking the Mudflow of Kantz Creek.

7.0 Longmire Park Headquarters and Visitors Center (2761): food and lodgings, rest rooms. Vistas of Mount Rainier.

Mount Rainier.

9.0 Cougar Rock Campground.
11.0 Christine Falls (3676): drinking water out of mountainside. As you go higher the area is more open and alpine
in setting. Vistas include snow-patched mountains, waterfalls, streams and wonderful expanses of protected forests.
12.0 Cross Nisqually River (3900). Above is the Nisqually
Glacier and its mudflow course.
13.0 Take viewpoint road to the right. Magnificent overlooks
of Tatoosh Range (6-7000).
14.0 Rejoin highway again to Paradise.
14.5 Canyon Rim (4462).
16.5 Junction (4800): keep right. Left takes you to Paradise
(5400): Visitors Center and campground. Road levels off

here. Easy biking as you start down through alpine scenery. Lakes and vistas of Mount Rainier from another side. The gorge of Stevens Canyon with its road winding alongside the mountain side. This spectacular downhill run is serious business. There are places where a spill from your bike could mean your end over a cliff! Take your time; this road barely hangs on the side of these cliffs. Two tunnels here.

24.3 Box Canyon Picnic Area, then road levels off.

25.2 Cross Nickel Creek (2926). Views of Mt. Adams (12,307).

27.0 Start climbing again; very long.

29.0 Backbone Overlook: vista of Mount Rainier. Then start down again.

34.0 Cross Falls Creek (2225).

34.4 Grove of Patriarchs: a section of the forest that is about 1000 years old.

34.5 Cross Ohanapecosh River (2176), then come to a right on State 123, 1½ miles to the Ohanapecosh Campground and Visitors Center. End of second day: 36 miles.

0.0 *Third day* leave campground headed north on State 123.

1.5 Road to Paradise goes left as you start climbing through a stand of giant trees in the Grove of the Patriarchs.

3.8 Cross Panther Creek (2370). Stiff climbing beyond here with vistas of Mount Rainier. This is the longest, steady climb of the tour: 12 miles.

6.0 Drinking water off rock face.

8.0 Cross Deer Creek (3590).

9.0 Vistas of Mount Rainier behind Cowlitz Chimneys.

12.0 Cayuse Pass (4700). Left on State 410 and drop down for the next 40 miles alongside the White River. This is a good road with a narrow paved section for biking.

15.5 Road to Sunrise: Visitors Center, food and lodging, camping. This is a 15 mile ride with a 3400 to 6400 feet gain. An alternate here is to add another day and make your overnight stop at Sunrise: camping, food and lodgings. This is the best place from which to view Mount Rainier.

20.0 Crystal Mountain Recreation Area. Rough road here.

21.0 Silver Springs Campground, then a lodge, store and cafe.

22.0 Motel.

Flowered bluff above Pacific Ocean.

27.0 Campground. Good road from here; shoulder for biking in heavy traffic. Logging trucks.

29.5 Good paved shoulder as you pass through Snoqualmie National Forest where Weyhauser has stripped the mountains for miles.

34.0 Cafe, then another; then a store and motel as you come in alongside the White River.

34.5 Cafe, then lose good biking shoulder.

35.5 Federation Forest Interpretive Center: interesting exhibits and information.

46.5 Road to Mud Mountain Dam (2 miles).

50.0 Outskirts of Enumclaw: full services.

51.0 Fork in road; keep on State 164.

51.5 Junction of State 164/164Y. End of trip.

TOUR 42

Cool rain forests, a scenic shoreline, snow patched mountain background, alpine lakes, picturesque port towns and shore villages are parts of what help make this an exciting tour of the Olympic Peninsula. Places like the lakes west of Port Angeles, the parks along the Pacific Ocean, and the ride along the Hood Canal will make an unforgetable impression.

Location   Western Washington.

Season   Year round, but be prepared for cold, wet weather at anytime.

Transportation   Airlines and buses to Hoquiam and Port Angeles.

Rating   Mostly easy hills and flat biking with some stiff rises. Roads are generally good with long sections of good paved shoulders for biking. Traffic is usually light but there are logging trucks to worry about. This is an easy to moderate tour.

Reference   Write for map-brochure, Superintendent, Olympia National Park, 600 East Park Avenue, Port Angeles, Washington 98362. Also write for map-brochure: Forest Supervisor, Olympia National Forest, Federal Building, Olympia, Washington 98501.

Tour Outline   296 miles, loop tour: 4 days, 3 nights.
Hoquiam is a port town on Grays Harbor. Full services here; bicycle shops. Start tour in town at

- 0.0 Junction of State 109 and US 101. The airport is 2½ miles west via State 109 and Adams Street. Head north on US 101, through a commercial/residential area. All services here. Or go south on US 101 to center of Hoquiam.
- 0.5 Exhibit of logging engine. Easy road for biking. Traffic is heavy here on wide road. Shoulders can be biked, but you are going to eat a lot of dust as loggers pass.
- 4.0 Motel, cafe.
- 4.3 Road left to beaches. Traffic lessens as you follow alongside old logging canal. Wooded setting, scattered homes, Easy biking on long grades.
- 5.5 Cross West Branch Hoquiam River.
- 6.0 Beach road.

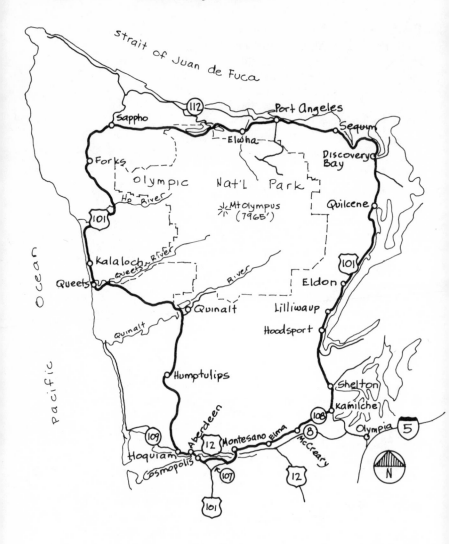

6.8 Cross West Branch Hoquiam River. Forest setting; few signs of farms or homes. Logging operations everywhere. Some vistas of Olympic Mountains. Also cedar shake mills along here on US 101.

8.0 Cafe, tavern, groceries.

10.5 Cross Humptulips River into the town of Humptulips. Store, cabins and campground to left.

13.7 Rest area: toilets. Steam engine exhibit.

28.2 Newberry Creek Road.

29.0 Start long downhill into Olympic National Forest.

31.0 National Fish Hatchery road.

33.0 First glimpse of snow patched Olympic Mountain peaks as you come into Neilton: store. Beyond here it is the tall forest as you pass through Quinalt Natural Area.

36.2 Road to Quinalt: full services and four campgrounds, about 2 miles.

37.2 Cross Quinalt River into Amanda Park: store, motel, cafe. Rough road out of here and more hills.

39.0 Road goes right to Quinalt Lake: drive-in eating.

40.3 Cabins, lunch. Tall forest beyond here; scenic biking.

47.7 West Boundary Road goes right.

49.7 Cross Raft River.

54.3 Queets Valley Road goes right. This takes you into the Rain Forest alongside Queets River. Take this in as far as you like. The dirt road can be biked.

61.0 Enter into Queets: cafe, store, laundromat.

61.5 Cross Queets River. Good road with shoulder for biking as you head for,

63.0 Pacific Ocean. A very beautiful area as you pass through Olympic National Park. Many trails lead down to the water. Parking areas for vistas are often equipped with toilets.

63.5 Primitive camping. Turn in here for view of ocean and coastline. Toilets here. Beyond here the beach trails start.

66.3 Ranger station.

66.5 Kalaloch Beach Ocean Village: food and lodgings.

67.0 Campground.

0.0 *Second day* continue north along coast. Vistas. Pass several more beach trails.

4.0 Road right leads to World's Largest Cedar. It's a big one!

6.7 Pass Rocky Beach Parking Area. Road swings away from beach to a climb inland. Shoulder for biking. Remote setting with hills.

12.0 Cross Nolan Creek.

17.0 Store, cafe.

18.0 Cross Hoh River.

18.5 Road to Oil City.

19.7 Road to Rain Forest alongside Hoh River.

26.5 Store, campground, motel. Then cross Bogachiel River to pass Bogachiel State Park: camping.

32.0 Forks: full services. Good road beyond here with biking shoulder.

33.0 Cross Calawah River.

33.5 Road left to La Push and Olympic National Park beach area.

36.0 Cross Soleduck River. Area is more open here; some farms.

40.5 Store at Lake Pleasant.

41.0 Campground. Vistas beyond here.

43.2 Cross Soleduck River, then rest area: toilets. Then cross Soleduck River again to enter Sappho: cafe. Road leads left to Neah Bay. Road heads east now.

45.7 Camping, cafe. Then cross Bean Creek.

49.0 Enter Olympic National Forest in the valley of the Soleduck River. Ridge on left.

51.2 Cross Soleduck River, then a campground.

52.0 Cross Soleduck River.

58.5 Enter Olympic National Park on long downhill to Lake Crescent surrounded by mountains. The lake is 624 feet deep.

60.0 Campground at west end of lake: food, lodgings, store. Scenic drive around lake through rain forest setting. Shady biking.

66.5 Crescent Lodge: food and lodgings.

67.0 Storm King Visitor Center: toilets. Beyond here you climb above the lake, then drop down to pass Lake Sutherland. a resort area. Vistas.

71.5 Restaurant, then resort cottages.

73.2 Cross Indian Creek and still going down.

74.0 Motel and drive-in eating.

76.0 Cross Indian Creek again.

77.5 Elwha River. Camping, cabins, laundromat, store and showers here. Road goes right of river to park campgrounds, 3-4 miles.

0.0 *Third day* continue on US 101, a stiff climb up out of the river valley to overlook Aldwell Lake.

2.0 Top rise, then drop to start another.

2.5 Top rise, then some short rise hills and vistas of the Straits of Juan de Fuca and Canada's Vancouver Island. Farms and scattered homes. Olympic Mountains in background. Straight ahead you can see the snow capped peaks of the Cascades on the mainland. As you approach Port Angeles the setting is mostly commercial/residential. Food and lodgings here. Stay on US 101 through the city.

7.7 State 11 goes right to Olympic National Park Visitor Center and up to Hurricane Ridge (about 20 miles); over a mile-high ride. Camping halfway up here. Keep ahead to downtown Port Angeles: full services. Bicycle shops. Visit waterfront. Ferry to Victoria.

8.2 Right on US 101 through town on a 4-lane road.

12.6 Cross Morse Creek into countryside. Vistas of mountains and water.

13.2 2-lane road with long easy grades and then short rise hills in open countryside.

15.2 Campground.

16.6 Store.

17.0 Restaurant.

18.2 Cross McDonald Creek.

19.8 Campground.

21.2 Store, then drive-in eating place.

22.2 Cross Dungeness River. At some points you can see across to the mainland and the distant Cascades.

23.2 Pass through Sequim: full services. Beyond here you are biking in a forested setting alongside Sequim Bay.

28.6 Sequim Bay State Park: camping, showers. Old Blyn Highway will take you down to the water and later rejoin US 101.

30.5 Cafe and store as you go through Blyn and start uphill. Be sure to treat yourself to the seafood in these shore towns: crab meat, smoked salmon, shrimp, oysters, etc. Vistas of bays are very scenic. Some roads go down closer to the water here. Some are deadend roads.

36.0 Campground.

39.2 Lodge and motel on bay.

41.2 Discovery Bay: store and cafe. State 113 goes left to Port Townsend.

43.5 State 104 goes left.

44.7 Campground as you pass Crocker Lake. Scenic ride here amongst mountains.

52.5 Store, cafe and motel as you pass through Quilcene. Long steady climb out of Quilcene into Olympic National Forest.

55.0 Cross Quilcene River and enter into a forested ride up through the mountains. Logging trucks.

56.4 Campground as you pass through narrow gorge.

58.2 Top rise and then a long downhill.

59.0 Interesting junk store.

60.2 Vistas of Hood Canal and islands.

61.0 Campground, then store as you come alongside water.

63.2 Campground, then enter Brinnon: store and restaurant.

64.2 Cross Dosewallips River, then Dosewallips State Park: camping, showers.

65.2 Store.

66.2 Cafe. Forested ride continues with some long grades up and down.

67.7 Cross Duckabush River. As you cross these streams and rivers emptying into the Hood Canal it is usually at a small scenic bay. Open views of islands and distant Cascades as you ride and drop to these small bays; some tough biking the next few miles.

69.7 Cross McDonald Creek.

70.8 Cross Fulton Creek.

71.7 Campground, laundromat.

72.4 Cabins, store.

74.6 Motel.

75.4 Beached boat.

76.0 Eldon: store, cafe, motel. Look for homemade pies in these shore villages. End of third day. Overnight can be spent in any of the campgrounds or motels in this area.

0.0 *Fourth day* continue south to

0.6 Cross Hamma Hamma River. Pleasant stretches of open biking along the water.

2.2 Cross Forested Creek.

2.5 Campground.

5.4 Cross Eagle Creek: public beach and toilets.

6.7 Public beach as you come into Lilliwaup: store, motel.

9.4 Motel, store, cafe, campground. More homes in this area as you approach Hoodsport.

10.4 Shell museum, cafes, motels.

12.2 Hoodsport: full services. This is a fishing town. Beyond here you pass a number of commercial services as you get closer to Shelton. More homes also. Fruit stands, too.

14.2 Skykomish Indian Reservation.

14.7 Rest area: toilets.

17.0 State 106 goes left. Keep ahead and leave water.

19.2 Campground, drive-in eating. Then start climbing.

20.2 Rest area: toilets.

22.2 Vistas behind of Olympic Mountain as you pass through logged off area.

23.5 Rest area: toilets. Then come into Shelton: full services. Bicycle shops.

27.0 Downtown Shelton: State 3 goes left.

27.3 Fork: keep left and rise above city, looking down on city and port.

28.6 Cross Mill Creek into open country with farms.

31.2 4-lane highway with median: wide paved shoulder for biking.

32.0 Cafe.

32.7 Right on State 108 at Kamiche; rough gravel shoulder. The setting is wooded with some small farms and scattered homes as you bike through a valley. Scenic ride where trees overhang. Good chance of seeing deer. Light traffic; logging.

38.2 End of valley: climbing now through open forest. This is a small private forest that has been maintained to give a semblance of virgin forest. Very scenic. Road is better beyond here as you come into McCleary: full services.

43.7 Road goes left here to State 8. Keep ahead on road to Whites; store. Road is rough. Traffic is light in a rural setting: small farms and scattered homes. Busy State 8 is on your left. Some short-rise hills beyond here. U-pick farms here for fruit lovers. Beautiful gardens and wild-flowers.

50.0 Elma: full services. Beyond here the area is a mix of residential/commercial/rural as you go to

54.2 Satsop: store, drive-in eating, cafe.

54.6 Campground.

54.8 Cross Satsop River.

55.8 Brady: store might be in operation.

57.8 Wide shoulder for biking, then come into Montesano: full services. This town claims to be the birthplace of America's tree farms. The landscaped approach to town is certainly one of the best in America. Follow signs on Main Street to freeway. Pass under the freeway and stay ahead on State 107 to

61.0 Cross Chehalis River. A narrow road; no shoulder. Short rise hills in a wooded setting. Scattered small farms and homes. Light traffic; logging.

63.3 Chehalis River on right.

64.8 Fork: keep right and drop down on a short cut to Aberdeen. Left will go up the hill 3 miles to US 101. Road now is a winding, hilly road through a wooded area.

67.0 The river still has the old logging piles used to store logs.

69.2 Right on US 101 into Cosmopolis and Aberdeen, passing through a very busy industrial/commercial/residential area. Full services for the next few miles. Bicycle shops here. Easy roads for biking through Aberdeen and Hoquiam.

71.7 Cross Chehalis River following signs left for Hoquiam. To beat the city traffic keep ahead a block or two and then go left. Roads will come back to US 101.

74.0 Enter Hoquiam.

75.6 Cross Hoquiam River and go right a block to State 109.

TOUR 43

This route takes bikers down the Columbia River to the Pacific Ocean, then heads north to bend around the Willapa Hills and head back inland. Very scenic biking on ridge tops and at seaside. Vistas of Rainier, Mt. St. Helens and Mt. Adams on first day.

Location   Southwest Washington.

Season   Year-round.

Transportation   Bus to Kelso.

Rating   Good roads with mostly light traffic. Long sections with wide shoulder for biking. The terrain is generally flat to hilly with some tough ones thrown in. An easy to moderate tour.

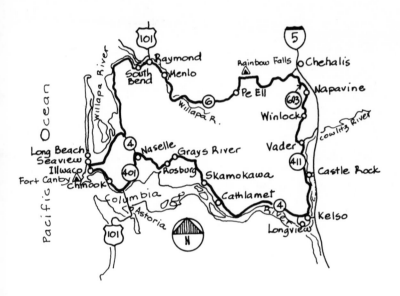

Tour Outline   208 miles, loop tour: 3 days, 2 nights.
Kelso is a large town with full services; bicycle shops. Start tour at junction of State 4/411. Take a

- 0.0   Left on State 4 for Longview, then after a block go right on State 4 to Long Beach in a very busy residential/commercial area. Easy biking here on wide shoulders. Heavy traffic as the area becomes part rural. Hills in background.
- 5.5   Cross Germany Creek; traffic is lighter. Some big trucks. Road is wide with poor shoulder. Columbia River is on left (canal used for log storage).
- 9.5   Columbia River: store. Scenic views of river and hills of Oregon on opposite shore. Lewis and Clark traveled along here in 1805 in their search for the Pacific Ocean. At points the route is cut out of orange cliffs as it winds

west along the river. Many accesses to water; some beach spots. Many ups and downs as you cross over headlands and drop into bays where streams empty into Columbia River. Some cliff rides and some wide shoulders for biking.

12.0 Cross Abernathy Creek.

14.0 Beach area.

16.0 Top rise. Columbia River has islands in it.

20.5 Motel.

21.3 Rest area.

21.5 Paved shoulders.

23.2 Drive-in eating.

24.0 State 409 goes left to Cathlamet: full services. Museum.

24.5 State 407 goes right.

25.8 Cross river. Route beyond here is flat and easy biking on wide shoulders.

30.0 Skamokawa: store, restaurant. Turn away from the river here and head into a valley. Farmlands.

33.5 Start climb out of the valley with a climbing lane; bike and hike over K. M. Mountain.

36.5 K. M. Mountain (1670). Then a long downhill with shoulder.

39.5 Cross Grays River.

40.0 As road starts up again look down on left: Grays River Covered Bridge.

41.0 Restaurant.

41.5 Grays River: store and tavern.

43.5 State 403 goes left. Rosburg: store. Leave the Grays River Valley and head due west. Clear cutting scenes.

47.5 Cross Deep River; paved shoulder.

48.6 Start climb. Top rise and drop down to

50.5 Rest area: toilets. Very scenic area by stream.

51.5 Naselle: motels, stores, cafe. Hand-carved furniture shop: Fishermen and Wives. Nice community. Then cross Naselle River.

53.3 Left on State 401: cafe. Road is easy biking on paved shoulder. Other roads to Naselle. Cross Naselle River again.

58.3 Cross Bean Creek. Traffic is light beyond here.

60.2 Long downhill to Columbia River where river remains along shore. Astoria, Oregon is across river. Road is cut out of cliffs. Lots of driftwood here.

62.0 On right: wreck of large ship, wooden timbers almost obscured by water and foliage now growing out of hull.

63.7 Rest area: toilets and information about area.

65.0 State 401 ends. Continue ahead on US 101. Left leads across bridge to Astoria. Traffic is moderate here as cars come off the bridge.

65.4 Campground: some scattered homes.

66.5 Historic point: Lewis and Clark Camp. Just beyond here you pass through a tunnel: walk bike through on pedestrian sidewalk.

68.0 Chinook: full services, interesting waterfront. Campground here on water.

68.6 Camping.

71.2 Camping left one mile.

73.2 Cross Wallicutt River. Campground.

73.5 Road goes right to Raymond. Keep ahead. Make one last rise and drop into Ilwaco, a resort-fishing town: full services.

76.5 Right on US 101 for Seaview and Long Beach. Straight ahead 3 mile to Fort Canby State Park: camping, showers. There are also a number of campgrounds in the area after turning north on US 101. Motels in the area.

0.0 *Second day* continue north through Ilwaco. The setting is commercial/residential with many services.

0.5 Camping right at fork in road.

1.2 Campgrounds left and right.

1.7 State 103 goes ahead to Long Beach, a resort area. Keep right on US 101 away from ocean on a rough road. Traffic is moderate.

4.0 Road to Astoria goes right: cafe.

5.4 Start long grade up through logged area.

6.0 Top rise and then down to

7.7 Cross Bear River and begin long drive around Willapa Bay. Light traffic on a good winding road. Easy biking in a very scenic tidewater setting. Willapa National Wildlife Refuge here.

12.0 Headquarters of Willapa National Wildlife Refuge.

14.0 Cross Naselle River and bike alongside river.

16.4 Left on US 101. State 4 goes ahead. Climb away from shore on a stiff climb.

17.0 Top rise.

18.0 Cross Nemah River. Short rise hills here in some forested setting.

21.0 Rest area: toilets, short rise hills here.

22.4 North Nemah River as you come back to bay again.

23.0 Lunch room at gas station. Long grades again as you ride along Willapa Bay in open country.

29.4 Cross Palex River.

32.0 Cross Boone River. More hills now as you skirt Willapa Bay and its river from the mountains.

35.0 Camping.

40.0 South Bend: full services in this part of town. Traffic is busy from here to Raymond.

42.0 Rest area: then soon enter into Raymond outskirts. This port town has full services.

44.4 Cross bridge and go right on State 6 to leave town through a residential area on a winding, hilly road.

46.6 Store, then drop down on a valley road. Vistas.

50.4 Menlo: store.

51.2 Cross Willapa River.

52.0 Good shoulder for biking on valley road.

55.4 Trap Creek, then start climb out of valley.

56.2 Fish hatchery: big farms here.

58.0 Cross Willapa River and enter Leban: store.

60.4 Cross Fern Creek, then come into Frances. Long grades up through forested setting to,

65.4 Bridge over RR tracks, then downhill through forest.

68.4 Bridge over RR tracks. Still going down through farm-lands and scattered homes.

70.2 Cross Chehalis River and enter into Pe Ell: stores, cafe. Shoulder for biking out of town into forest.

76.0 Mt. Rainier views.

77.0 Road to Dryad.

78.0 Rainbow Falls State Park: camping.

0.0 *Third day* keep east on State 6 alongside Chehalis River. Vistas of Mt. Rainier ahead. The setting remains a mix of forest and open farmlands. Some scattered homes. Long grades.

7.3 Cross South Fork Chehalis River. On left is abandoned

covered bridge. Around the bend there is a dirt road on left leading down to it.

9.0 Chehalis River on left below. Vistas of Mt. Rainier.

11.0 Store as you cross Chehalis River.

13.2 Right on State 603. Just beyond here on State 6 you can visit the historic church and cemetery at Claquato. The church was built in 1858. The village was an important stop off on the route from Columbia River to Puget Sound. Cross the Chehalis River onto a narrow country road through large farms. Some scattered homes with beautiful gardens. Light traffic on some steep short rise hills that take you up to a ridge and great vistas. On a clear day Mt. Rainier, Mt. St. Helens and Mt. Adams are in view. Easy biking along here amongst the woods and wildflowers.

18.2 Power substation.

20.0 Napavine: store, cafe. More hills beyond here.

23.2 Railroad alongside. Forest is more apparent as the ridge route is left behind.

26.0 Cross Olequa Creek and enter into Winlock, an old mill town: full services. Winlock has the world's largest egg displayed in its town park!

26.8 Rather than follow the signs across the RR tracks to I-5 continue ahead on the Winlock-Vader Road. Cross the creek and at a fork keep left. This is a mostly downhill run in a narrow valley passing small farms and scattered homes alongside a creek. Light traffic.

33.0 Left on State 506 for Vader. Climb a hill out of town and take a

34.0 Right on State 411. Open farmlands with more vistas now. Road is rough; short-rise hills with very light traffic.

36.0 Cross Olequa Creek. Road is in a wooded area in sight of creek. Access to creek for swimming or picnicking if you like.

40.8 Good road, then a long downhill to Castle Rock, passing orchards.

42.7 Contemporary structure: Castle Rock High School.

43.0 Road goes left to Castle Rock: store. At fork in road keep left. Forested ride on an easy grade.

44.8 Vistas of valley and I-5.

45.8 Cowlitz River on left. Scattered homes.

49.5   Riverside park.
49.8   Store.
52.5   Kelso city limits. Pass under a bridge and go
53.0   Right on State 411 to
53.4   State 4 and end of tour.

WYOMING

Wyoming is a splendid land. The very best in mountains, forest-
lands, canyons, prairies, grasslands, lakes and streams are found
here. And it is a historied land. More than any other western
state the wagon trains, stage runs, cattle drives, and before them
the explorers, crossed the Wyoming Territory. Today bikers can
view many of the same wonders seen by those first pioneers. The
Devils Tower in northeastern Wyoming. The Medicine Bow
Mountains and the wild mustangs in the southeast. Flaming Gorge
in the southwest. The Bighorn mass in the north central region,
and the splendor of the Tetons and Yellowstone in the northwest.
This is all mile-high country with lots of sunshine and cool summer days.

For more information about Wyoming write the Wyoming
Travel Commission, 2320 Capitol Avenue, Cheyenne, Wyoming
82001.

TOUR 44

Touring the Grand Teton and Yellowstone National Parks is un-
doubtedly one of the finest outings in America. You must take
your time! If possible incorporate a tram ride up to Rendezvous
Peak, a float trip on the Snake, or a hike into the Teton Peaks.
There is no one place here in which you will be disappointed.
Note: possible overnight stops are not suggested for these tours.
Ample accommodations do exist, allowing for easy tailoring of
mileage to suit individual preferences.

Location   Northwest Wyoming.

Season   Spring, summer and fall. July and August is the busy
season.

Jackson Lake.

Transportation   Bus and airlines to Jackson.

Rating   Tour 44 is the easier of the two. Mostly the roads are in good condition. The terrain must be considered mountain biking with some bike and hike sections: Lewis Canyon and crossing the Continental Divide. However these elevation gains are seldom more than 1,000 feet. Traffic is heavy on all roads at all times, but it is slow and aware of many bikers.

Reference   Write for map-brochure: Superintendent, Grand Teton National Park, Moose, Wyoming 83012. Also write, Superintendent, Yellowstone National Park, Wyoming 82190. Topo maps also available from the same addresses.

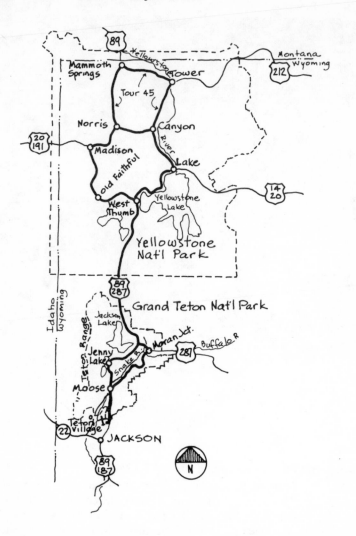

Tour Outline   228 miles, loop tour: 4 to 5 days.
Jackson is a small town with full services. As a vacation place
it has enough going on to keep visitors busy for a week. Hiking,
boating, fishing, horseback riding and many other outdoor activities here. The town also has good eating places, theaters and fine

shops. Take the tram from Teton Village to Rendezvous Peak (10,446). Magnificent view of Jackson Hole. Start the tour at Jackson Airport, 8½ miles north of town.

0.0 Exit airport and go north on US 26/89/187. Easy biking on road that is quite level here in the Hole surrounded by mountain peaks. The open fields are flat to rolling covered with sage, grass and wildflowers.

3.5 Left goes to Visitors Center just a short distance away, passing Moose Enterprises with full service before crossing the Snake River to reach the center. Back on the highway continue north. There are several turnouts with views of mountains and Snake River.

11.5 Snake River Overlook; excellent view of Snake River winding below. Look for rubber rafts carrying people down the river. Beyond here you start on a long downhill.

15.5 Road to Cunningham Cabins.

16.8 Cross Spread Creek.

20.3 Cross Buffalo River just above its confluence with the Snake River.

20.5 Left on US 89/287 to the Buffalo Entrance Station. Fee here is good for Grand Tetons and Yellowstone Parks. This is the beginning of an easy climb, out of the Hole alongside the Snake River.

24.3 Road goes left to Jenny Lake (a section of your return trip).

25.3 Jackson Lodge road: food and lodgings. Beyond here the road has a paved shoulder for a while. Setting is more wooded now.

27.2 Cross Pilgrim Creek.

29.5 Colter Bay Village: full services, camping. Soon some great views of Jackson Hole with the Tetons in the background. More climbing now as you get into short rise hills.

37.0 Lizard Creek Campground. Then the first tough hill followed by a good downhill run.

43.7 Snake River Campground, then the Flagg Ranch with full services.

44.6 Huckleberry Hot Springs: full services, camping.

46.5 South Entrance (6866). Enter Yellowstone National

Park and begin a long uphill climb to West Thumb along-side the Lewis River. Some bike and hike.

50.5 Lewis Canyon; a spectacular ride here: waterfalls, lush valleys, plunging canyon walls.

51.5 Top the climb from South Entrance.

53.5 There are spots along here where you can go down to the river as it meanders through meadows. Look for moose.

56.0 Cross Lewis River; falls here.

57.2 Lewis Lake Campground; then bike along Lewis Lake shore.

63.0 Continental Divide (7988).

65.2 Road to Grant Village: camping. Then views of Yellowstone Lake (7731).

67.0 Right to West Thumb (7784): store and restaurant. Steaming basins here at edge of lake. Keep right on going north around lake to Bridge Bay. This is easy biking alongside the lake. Pass more hot pools.

69.5 Start to rise above lake.

72.5 Paved shoulder for biking in this area.

81.5 Keep on main road or take a right on Gull Point Drive down along lakeshore. Then road to Natural Bridge.

83.0 Bridge Bay: camping.

85.0 Lake: full services. You leave the lake to follow down along the Yellowstone River.

86.6 US 14/20 goes right to Fishing Bridge and East Entrance. Keep ahead alongside Yellowstone River.

91.8 Black Dragon Cauldron and Mud Volcano. You can smell them! Then come into the very beautiful Hayden Valley, a broad, flat grassy, open countryside, sage on the hills and forest in background. Just before river goes into its canyon and you start climbing.

98.8 Road to Artist Point.

99.8 One-way road exiting from canyon overlook.

101.0 Canyon (7734): full services. Right here to take one-way road overlooking the very spectacular Grand Canyon of the Yellowstone River. Several overlooks and views of falls. One leads down to the edge of the falls.

103.0 Rejoin the highway and head back to Canyon junction.

106.4 Canyon junction. Left here for Norris on a flat road that is soon climbing. (*TOUR 45* continues straight ahead for

Tower.) Look for beaver dam and house in a pond on your right. Road has some paved shoulders on it.

107.4 Start climb.

108.3 Top rise and start a mostly downhill to Norris.

112.3 Long downhill.

114.0 Short uphill.

114.6 Long downhill with paved shoulders alongside Gibbon River.

117.4 Norris: campground to the right about 1 mile. Go left for Madison on a mostly downhill run. You are still following the Gibbon River. Good chance for seeing moose or elk.

122.0 Beryl Spring. Road narrows and winds into Gibbon River Canyon.

125.3 Gibbon Falls, then a sharp downhill run to pass some springs and then reach,

130.0 Madison (6806): camping. Confluence of Gibbon and Firehole Rivers that form the Madison River. Road now is uphill on easy grade alongside Firehole River. Note: 3 of America's greatest rivers have their beginnings in this mountainous region. The Madison becomes the Missouri; the Snake is headwaters for the Columbia and the Green River leads into the Colorado.

137.0 Geyser basins from here on to Old Faithful.

138.6 Firehole Lake Drive goes left.

143.2 Cross Firehole River.

144.8 Right to Old Faithful: full services here. Museum, programs. Good road beyond here.

146.4 Cross Firehole River and start stiff climbing to cross the Continental Divide at,

152.2 Craig Pass (8262), then a downhill only to start up again to again cross the

157.8 Continental Divide (8391).

161.0 Yellowstone Lake.

161.5 Left to West Thumb. Keep right and return the way you started. A downhill run mostly to South Entrance, then some up, then a long downhill another 43 miles to Jackson Lake and a

204.2 Right to Jenny Lake, easy biking with Tetons in view.

205.5 Jackson Lake Dam.

206.6 Chapel of Sacred Heart, then Signal Mountain: full services, camping.

212.5　After a sharp curve left take a right to Jenny Lake; one-way, rough road.

215.2　Junction. Ahead is String Lake and a stream connecting to Jenny Lake. Go left. Just beyond here is Jenny Lake Lodge.

216.5　Jenny Lake.

217.5　Moose Village: tent camping.

218.0　Right on road to Visitor Center and Jackson.

221.0　In distant left is the yellow scar of the Gros Ventre slide where the mountain slid down to make a lake on the Gros Ventre River. It later burst leaving a smaller lake.

221.5　Cross Cottonwood Creek.

224.0　Menors Ferry; Chapel of the Transfiguration.

224.7　Visitors Center: store here. Then cross Snake River and take a

225.3　Right to airport.

228.8　Airport. Another 8½ miles to Jackson.

TOUR 45

This is a tough one on the sections from Canyon to Tower and just south of Mammoth to Kingman Pass.

Tour Outline　　270 miles, loop tour: 5 to 6 days.
Start this tour as in *TOUR 44* but at Canyon continue ahead rather than go left for Norris.

106.4　Canyon junction. Keep ahead on a stiff climb for Dura-ven Pass. Some bike and hike here in alpine scenery that is spectacular. Vistas of snow patched peaks.

108.7　Durraven Pass (8859). Then along downhill with some ups in it as you bike down alongside Mt. Washburn (10,243) to join the canyon of the Yellowstone and then

119.4　Tower (6264): food and lodgings and camping. Soon US 212 comes in from right and you climb out of the basin to

122.4　Top rise.

122.8　Road to Petrified Tree, a short run to a very interesting exhibit. Then a series of long up and downs through lava flow country.

124.4　Floating Island Lake.

134.5　Cross Lava Creek, then a long downhill along the creek canyon. Soon the white bulge of the hot springs are in view on the mountainside.

136.0 Cross Gardiner River, then climb back up to Mammoth Hot Springs: full services. Museum.

138.0 Left on US 89 through the services area. Access to the hot springs here. Then a steep climb above the town. Good vistas. Soon you're alongside the top of the springs; access here. Keep climbing on to top the rise and

141.0 Pass through large boulder field.

142.0 Canyon narrows; road is notched out of cliffs. Rustic Falls and Swan Lake at Kingmans Pass. This is plateau country with open fields and easy biking on a poor road. Very scenic.

145.5 Cross Gardiner River with its beginnings in this plateau. Watch for moose and elk in the ponds and marshes.

146.0 Campground.

148.6 Appollinaris Springs; water.

150.0 Obsidian Cliffs and keep alongside Obsidian Creek to pass Twin Lakes, some springs, then a

157.0 Campground.

157.8 Road to Canyon goes left. Join *TOUR 44* here for another 111½ miles to airport. 270 miles.